Waking Up Work

Waking Up Work

USING MINDFULNESS TO UNCOVER THE
UNKNOWNS AND DO THE RIGHT THING

By

Timothy R. Velner

ISBN: 979-8-638-50847-0 (paperback)

www.wakingupwork.com

Table of Contents

Preface

When I first began to practice law in the mid-1990s, I was a fish out of water. I was the only guy in our law firm who wore something other than a white shirt and tie. I wore a blue shirt and tie. If someone was looking for me, the response usually, with an eye roll, was, "Just look for the guy in the colored shirt."

I didn't enjoy my job, but I needed to work. I had student loans and a mortgage. Gradually, however, I grew discontent. I was young, single, and living the life of a man in a midlife crisis. I often found myself thinking, *What are you doing? You're stuck at a job that does nothing more than provide a paycheck.*

I repeatedly wondered, *What is my purpose for working here? To review documents and make money? There has got to be more to life. I can't just keep doing this to do it—for a paycheck.*

Finally, the discontent grew to a point that my sanity demanded change. I sold my house and with the profit paid off my student loans. I was free to explore.

I've always been intrigued by the question of purpose: *What are we all doing here? There has got to be more to life than making money, competition, and checking the boxes.*

I was intrigued by the elephant in the room: *What is our purpose for being here?*

I wanted to dig deeper. I applied to Divinity School in Berkeley, California, was accepted, and was on my way to a new adventure. I knew I didn't want to be a minister, but I was compelled to scratch my itch. I loved Divinity School. I loved being in an environment with people who were seekers, interested in the same topics as me. I loved the diversity of thought, perspective, and life experience.

But I also realized something quite quickly. Contemplating philosophy and purpose in a vacuum is easy and stale. Living philosophy and purpose in the hectic world is a whole other animal. I enjoyed contemplating questions of the unknown, but what I wanted/needed was to live contemplation through the complexity of life. I wanted to bring purpose to action. I wanted to bring purpose to work.

But how was I to do that? Church was for Sundays and to be kept out of the work environment, and philosophy and purpose were personal matters. Work was work and life was life. No mixing the two. Dead end. Or so I thought.

A series of events, however, pushed me to start intermixing the two. My son was born with cognitive challenges, and my daughter started to struggle with mental illness in her early teens. I no longer had the ability to separate work from life. These events threw our family into a new universe of perspective. I didn't see the world through the same lens anymore. I soon learned that this unique perspective if not shared imposed a heavy burden. But if shared, it provided value…to others. I began to tell my story, and the more I did, the more others began to tell their stories. The stories provided insight and fleshed out hidden information—information that was transformational if brought to light. I realized that we all have unique life purposes. Life purposes that often remain concealed and impose heavy burdens. But when shared, they provide value to others in the form of perspective.

Everyone has a unique story. Why are we keeping our stories to ourselves, particularly at work? If we are empowered to share our unique life experiences at work, we provide our companies with a plethora of tools in the form of differing perspectives to flesh out and tackle problems.

In a similar manner, the problems and issues we experience at work also provide unique perspectives to our personal lives. Unique perspectives that help frame our personal growth. Purpose from work and purpose from life when shared can be dual-win opportunities.

How do we do this? We do this through awareness. And the implementation of this awareness through courage, sharing, and vulnerability. I call it waking up work. We wake up our work by creating a purposeful company culture that encourages us to share our unique perspectives and ideas. That sharing, in turn, percolates company unknowns into awareness. And when unknowns are brought to light, we can make informed decisions, mitigate risk, and do the right thing.

Part 1

Right

Knowing what is right to do in the moment is difficult. It's easy when someone else tees it up for us but significantly more difficult when we are left to our own devices. As we will see from some interesting social psychology experiments described in later chapters, 90 percent of us routinely follow the lead of another—no questions asked. Ninety percent of us let right be determined by someone else. We see this with our companies, and we see it in culture.

Executives are often touting that their companies are entrenched in doing the right thing only to become exposed for not quite getting there, as we will further explore in later chapters. We see it in culture with George Floyd's situation where an officer ruthlessly detained an African American to the point of killing him. Three other officers stood nearby and did not intervene. There was a righteous outcry against the four officers and a major shift in cultural sediment in support of the Black community. Prior to the George Floyd incident, 17 percent of the population supported the Black Lives Matter movement. After the incident, that percentage increased to twenty-eight. Where were the 11 percent hiding before the incident? It's easy to join the bandwagon after the fact.

And what about the three officers who stood by and did nothing? It's convenient for us to sit in hindsight and righteously proclaim they should have intervened. But as we will see in coming chapters, going against the gravity of a situation is not only not easy, it is incredibly difficult.

Or COVID-19. How many self-proclaimed experts do we now have on the subject? Where were the experts before the pandemic occurred? The gravity of culture changed almost overnight, and so did the willingness to get on board without question and righteously shame those who did not. Many of those who did not jump on board were simply questioning the magnitude and impact of the response and that the right thing to do was not so black and white. It is often our default nature to jump on board with the gravity of the situation and what may be right at that particular moment. What is much more difficult is to be at the forefront—the first to see that unique action may be warranted in a particular situation.

There is no scripted formula for right through foresight, but there is often consensus around right in hindsight. This book will explore why right, and the appended risk, so easily becomes buried and lost. We will learn through a series of interesting social psychology experiments that 90 percent of us go through life sleepwalking and blindly succumb to situational gravity. We will see that unless we become and stay aware, our decisions will likely be directed by the forces of others.

Most importantly, we will learn that there is something we can do about it. We all have within us the power to guide our own creation, to wake up.

CHAPTER 1

Company Mission Statements

DOING THE RIGHT thing is difficult to define. What is right for one person may not be right for another. And what is right at one particular point in time may not be right at a later point in time. Right is context dependent, and context in society is constantly changing. The vague concept of right can lead to the term becoming trite, merely a nice sound bite with no substance. And too often we see this happen. For example, one well-publicized company went to great lengths to do the right thing. Its mission and vision include the following:

- Our vision has nothing to do with transactions, pushing products or getting bigger for the sake of bigness. It's about building lifelong relationships with one customer at a time…We strive to be recognized by our stakeholders as setting the standard among the world's great companies for integrity and principled performance. This is more than just doing the <u>right thing</u>. We also have to do it the <u>right way</u>.

- Our vision is at the center of our culture. It's important to our success, and frankly it's been probably the most significant contributor to our long-term performance. If I have one job here, its keeper of the culture.

This company also had safeguards in place to do the right thing. It had an ethics hotline and an ethics training program for its employees. It was listed among Gallup's Great Places to Work for multiple years, with employee engagement scores in the top quintile of US companies. It was ranked seventh on *Barron's* list of most respected companies. The CEO was named industry person of the year in 2013.

This same company was the darling of its industry, with a soaring stock price and some of the highest returns among its peers. One particular sector of the company was especially strong, with profits surging year after year. The head of that sector was at one time named the most powerful person in the industry.

But it turns out doing the right thing was not as important as process and profits. The company's CEO said one thing; the company's culture said another. The company had put so much pressure on its sales force to hit ever-increasing quotas for new accounts, many of the employees (hundreds of thousands) began to create fraudulent accounts to hit their numbers. This went on for multiple years. And it didn't go unnoticed by the rank and file as contrary to its cultural mission of doing the right thing.

As reported in the media, a note was sent to senior management from one employee: "Surely you must be aware that you will reach a sales number to be achieved that will force the staff to cheat to obtain it."

Tens of thousands of customers called the company to complain of errant accounts opened in their names. Eighty-five hundred employees were terminated over a period of five years for not hitting their quotas. The wife of one of the company executives complained to her husband after she was notified that two errant accounts were opened in her name. The executive raised the issue with the head of the sector and spoke of it around the company. The head of the sector, however, asked him to stop telling that story, as it didn't make the unit look good. The profit default was in firm control.

When the issue first came to light through the media, the CEO said it was the result of a few bad apples, that 99 percent of employees were doing the right thing. The company also initially stated that the lapses resulted from a breakdown among a small number of team members: "When we find lapses, we do something about it."

It turns out that hundreds of thousands of employees were engaged in this activity for fourteen years, and over two million unauthorized accounts were created. Doing the right thing was nowhere to be found. It had become a trite sound bite. What spoke louder and clearer was the culture of process and profits. A culture that had become the company's default mode of action.

A separate company in the same sector with a similar publicly stated mission was also recently shamed in the media. This company proclaimed that it empowered its employees to do the right thing. But when an employee tried to do what she and her supervisor thought was the right thing, she was fired for not following company process.

This employee was working at a call center during the Christmas season when a customer called to ask when the money he had recently deposited would be available for withdrawal. He indicated he had recently been at a branch location, and another employee had told him the money would be available the next day so he could buy Christmas presents for his nine- and ten-year-old kids. The customer was now stuck at a gas station because his debit card had insufficient funds due to the recently deposited money not being released. The call center employee said she would look into it and determined that his money was still not accessible. She felt bad and offered to bring him twenty dollars of her own money for gas. He said no, but she asked her supervisor if it would be OK if she drove the money to the man during her upcoming break. Her supervisor agreed and apparently gave the employee the twenty dollars for the man's gas.

When the bank officers found out about the situation, both the call center employee and her supervisor were fired. The company said they had broken with company process and put themselves and the customer at unnecessary risk. Company policy prohibited call center employees from meeting customers.

These two companies were publicly shamed in the media for doing-the-right-thing failures. They were essentially shamed for a culture of hypocrisy. But they are likely no different than the vast majority of companies. Establishing and maintaining a company culture that fights against society's default of prosperity and survival is extremely difficult. It takes constant awareness.

Doing the Right Thing (DTRT)

The underlying, default purposes of most companies are profit and survival. And because companies consist of an aggregate of individuals, there is often another default in play—process, the manner in which individual employees work together. The bare-bones structure for most companies is process, profits, and succession. These are typically the foundations upon which companies guide their decisions.

Companies will thus likely create at this level unless and until they decide otherwise. However, companies often want to set themselves apart and build into their culture other foundations, a popular one being doing the right thing (DTRT).

But what does DTRT mean?

Becoming Trite

DTRT often becomes trite because *right* is a lofty concept that is hard to define. In fact, it is almost impossible to define what is right. As we will see in later chapters, social psychologists have discovered through extensive research, investigation, and experiments that there is no universal concept of right—what is right depends on the context of the situation.

Doing what is right may be impossible to define, but common sense may dictate what it is not. Doing what is right is not creating/growing through the default; it implies something more than the minimum standard.

Doing what is right means that a company has proclaimed its decisions will not automatically be governed by the defaults of process, profits, and survival. Rather its decisions, and hence its evolution, will be guided by an awareness of myriad factors.

But this does not remove the potentially trite element of doing what is right in a company's culture. It's a nice sound bite, but it will remain trite unless and until those within the company believe it's personally beneficial to them. After all, we are ultimately governed by self-interest. We may at times act outside our self-interest, but that is usually short lived. To make the culture of doing what is right lasting, those within the company must believe that it is personally beneficial to them.

As we will explore in the following chapters, companies that can establish a culture of making decisions outside of the default are likely to become magnets for employees who value purposeful growth and doing what is right.

CHAPTER 2

Mitigating Risk and Unknown Unknowns

I'VE WORKED AS an attorney managing litigation and company risk for more than twenty-five years. One question I'm frequently asked is what is the biggest risk that companies face. There is no shortage of risk for companies, from ever-expanding regulatory issues; poorly selected partners; scope creep; new and quicker processes; ever-changing technology; quicker, cheaper, faster; more complicated design; unforeseen conditions; and unknown market conditions. The list goes on, but there is typically one underlying element to all of the risks. That underlying element was summed up in 2001 by Donald Rumsfeld. Rumsfeld, then US Secretary of Defense, was asked what he thought the greatest threat was to the United States in the War on Terror. He responded with the following statement:

There are known knowns.
There are known unknowns.
It's the unknown unknowns that pose the biggest threat.

He took a lot of heat in the media for this statement as fancy wordplay, similar to Bill Clinton's, "It depends on what the meaning of the word 'is' is."

But what Rumsfeld stated is common sense. Known risks can be solved. Risks that we know we don't know can be explored, made known, and solved. It is just a matter of effort and resources for each. But unknown unknowns are where the problems lie. If we don't know what we don't know, the risks never hit our radars; no amount of resources or effort will help.

The question then becomes: How can we create a company culture to uncover the unknown unknowns?

The answer to that question will ultimately lead toward better risk mitigation and a greater likelihood of doing the right thing. But before we begin to uncover the unknown unknowns, let's take a step back to see how they got that way.

Next, we will explore anecdotally and through social psychology an extremely interesting, and apparently inherent, aspect of human behavior: that most, *but not all*, of us are essentially programmed to follow and blindly accept the default of the current culture. Part 3 will investigate the personal defaults by which we commonly, and often blindly, make decisions. Part 4 will then take us through twenty-six separate tools by which we as individuals, and collectively as companies, can endeavor to create a culture to raise awareness, mitigate risk, and do the right thing.

PART 2

Purpose and the 10 Percent

Chapter 3

Philosophy: What's the Point Anyway?

Four professionals are standing around a coffee bar, conversing about whose profession provides the most value to society.

The chemist proudly professes, "Of course it's mine. Without understanding the elements of nature, we couldn't evolve. Without chemists, we'd be living in the stone ages."

The physicist chimes in, "Elements are fine, but without understanding how they interrelate, we could not advance. It's the interaction that matters. And without us, there is not advancement."

The philosopher then proudly proclaims, "That's all fine and dandy, but without understanding why—"

At that moment, the fourth member of the group, the biologist, interrupts the philosopher and says, "Would you shut the f—— up and get back to making our coffee."

As the joke implies, philosophy may be an interesting subject, but there is no money in it. Most people conceive of it is an intellectual pursuit with no practical effect. Philosophers at the end of the day simply end up being very talkative baristas—or even worse, lawyers.

I love philosophy. It is the elephant in the room that very few of us like to acknowledge or, God forbid, discuss. What in the heck are all of us doing here on this round object called Earth? To many, it is not worth engaging in the process because there will never be any answer; it is just a waste of mental energy. It may be a good conversation piece, but to what end?

Regardless of the biologist's insistence that the philosopher shut the f—— up and get back to his job as a barista making coffee, I propose that the single most important question you will ever ask, *or more likely not ask,* is, "What is my purpose for being here?"

Whether you ask that question, and how often you do so, will be the primary factor in creating the environment in which you evolve and grow. In other words, it will set your default and create your culture.

CHAPTER 4

The Hero

WE'VE ALL HEARD stories or read about people being mugged in broad daylight while strangers pass them by and do nothing. It's called the "bystander effect" and based on the principle that individuals are less likely to intervene in a situation when others are around. The greater the number of bystanders, the less likely it is that one of them will help. The 1964 murder of Kitty Genovese led social psychologists John Darley and Bibb Latane to first study this effect in 1968.

Kitty was a twenty-eight-year old woman who was stabbed outside across the street from her apartment building in Queens, New York. Two weeks after the murder, the *New York Times* published an article claiming that thirty-eight witnesses saw or heard the attack and yet none of them called the police or came to her aid. In a similar incident in Richmond, California, a fifteen-year-old girl was brutally assaulted and raped outside a homecoming dance while as many as twenty witnesses watched without intervening. One of the police officers investigating the case commented, "What makes it even more disturbing is the presence of others. People came by, saw what was happening, and failed to report it."

Similar stories abound: people in a public situation are called to act yet do not step up.

These events and others prompted social psychologists to study this phenomenon in a multitude of experimental situations where they place a confederate (person in the study) in distress and the actions/inactions (do they intervene?) of strangers are noted and studied.

The results are consistently astounding: *It is the rare individual who will intervene; 90 percent of strangers do not stop to help.*

The act of nonintervention among 90 percent of people is astounding, but what I find to be more interesting is the 10 percent who do act. What causes the 10 percent to act? What is it about these 10 percent that is different?

The 10 percent have repeatedly been studied, and no easy conclusions have been reached. When asked why they act, the 10 percent typically respond, "I don't know. I just acted. There was just something in me that moved me."

We may not know exactly what makes the 10 percent different, but we do know some things. For whatever reason, the call to act in an ambiguous situation gets placed on their radar screen. The situational need for their intervention registers on their radar, while it does not for the remaining 90 percent.

We know this because when one variable in the stranger studies is changed, the nine-to-one ratio gets flipped: *When that one variable is changed, 90 percent of strangers will now intervene.*

What is that one variable?

When the victim is being attacked and he personally calls a stranger to action, "Hey, you in the blue shirt, please help me," 90 percent of the time the stranger called to intervene will help.

Hence when the situation is placed on our radars by someone else, 90 percent of us will act when needed. It's getting the situation on our radars that seems to be so difficult for the majority of us.

CHAPTER 5

The Milgram Memory Study

According to Stanford psychologist Philip Zimbardo in his book *The Lucifer Effect: Understanding How Good People Turn Evil,* following World War II and during the trials of some in the Nazi regime, a social psychologist from Yale University, Stanley Milgram, was curious about why so many German citizens did not intervene to stop the atrocities.

"How could those German citizens have allowed this to happen?"

The Holocaust could not have happened without the citizens' passive enablement. Why did they not step up and stop it? The answer has shone a light on human tendencies.

Milgram devised a groundbreaking study that reflected a fundamental element of human nature—the majority of people, in many cases 90 percent, will routinely, blindly follow authority and succumb to the pressure of the situation even when it means injury to another.

It is the rare person, one among about ten, who realizes on his own accord it's time to step up and go against the gravity of the situation.

In 1963, Milgram called for volunteers to participate in a "memory study." The study was noticed in a New Haven newspaper to the effect: "Looking for volunteers, between ages 20 and 50 to participate in a memory study. You will be paid $4.00 a day plus $.50 for your transportation. We are looking for people from all walks of life, carpenters, doctors, lawyers, secretaries, laborers."

Only students were excluded from the study. The volunteers were told they were to be "teachers" helping other "volunteers" increase their memory through negative reinforcement. The negative reinforcement was based upon an escalating series of shocks. The volunteer "learners" were not in fact volunteers but rather confederates whom the teacher volunteers were told were part of the study. The volunteers drew straws to see who would act as teachers. The drawing was rigged so that the actual volunteers would always draw the teacher straws.

The learners were placed in a separate room and hooked up to a shock machine. The teachers were told that they were to administer increasing shocks to the learners every time they gave an incorrect response or no response to a series of memory-recall questions. The confederate learners were not actually hooked up to the shock machine, but the teachers did not know this.

In the teacher's separate room was the shock apparatus. It involved a series of thirty shock levels, from fifteen volts to 450 volts. The teachers were given a zap of forty-five volts to see what it felt like—a slight tingly pain. The machine had markings at various levels to indicate intensity:

- Tenth level (150 volts): strong shock
- Thirteenth level (195 volts): very strong shock
- Seventeenth level (255 volts): intense shock
- Twenty-first level (315 volts): extremely intense shock
- Twenty-fifth level (375 volts): danger—severe shock
- Twenty-ninth and thirtieth levels (435 and 450 volts): "XXX"

Standing next to the teacher was a "researcher" in a white lab coat who was running the study. The study began, and the learners initially provided correct responses to the memory-recall questions. The teachers were told to provide positive reinforcement through verbal praise: "Good job."

Soon the learners began giving incorrect responses, however. For each incorrect response, the teacher was required to administer a shock, with each subsequent answer requiring a higher shock level.

As the shocks grew in intensity, the learners complained of more and more discomfort. According to Zimbardo:

- At lower levels, learners complained of the shocks hurting.
- As levels increased, the learners began to scream, "Please stop!"
- The researcher in the white lab coat then pressed the teachers to continue.
- As the shocks intensified, the learners began to complain of heart conditions.
- As the errors continued, the pleas to stop intensified.

- The teachers pled with the learners to concentrate harder: "I don't want to have to shock you."
- Learner responded, "I can't stand the pain, let me out of here. You have no right to keep me here. I absolutely refuse to answer any more."
- At the twenty-second level (330 volts), the learners stopped responding, implying they may have passed out or possibly died.
- As the teachers grew reluctant to continue the escalation of shocks, the white-coated lab researchers urged them on:
  - After the first protest, the researcher said, "The experiment requires that you continue."
  - After the second protest, the researcher said, "It is absolutely essential that you continue."
  - After the third protest, the researcher said, "You have no other choice; you must go on."
  - After the fourth protest, the experiment was halted.

Prior to the study, Milgram had asked forty colleagues and graduate students to estimate how many teachers they thought would proceed all the way to 450 volts. They hypothesized that only 1 percent would go all the way because that was the percentage of sadists in society, and only a sadist would proceed to the final level. These colleagues also predicted that most teachers would discontinue the study after the tenth level (150 volts).

Their predictions were dead wrong and reflected a fundamental misunderstanding of human behavior at the time.

The actual results: Two-thirds of teachers proceeded all the way to 450 volts. More than 90 percent went all the way up to 330 volts—the point where learners stopped responding and were presumed to be unconscious.

This study has been replicated cross-culturally, cross-generationally, and across genders. The results are more or less consistent:

- Nine percent of people will conform to the situation, at the direction of "outside forces," to the point of harming another.
- Ten percent—and in many cases less than 10 percent—will go against the situational forces of the instructor and do what they feel is right.

The study seems to reflect something remarkable about human nature: we are essentially hardwired to follow the lead of those in authority.

What I find most interesting about the study is not only the incredible difficulty of proceeding against situational forces (i.e., culture) but also that something can be done to redirect these situational forces to cause the difficult to become the easy.

In the case of the stranger studies, changing one factor causes the inversion of the nine-to-ten ratio. Similarly, changing one element will cause 90 percent of the teachers to halt the experiment prior to 330 volts. In the referenced study, the teachers were participating alone; they were in a separate room with just the researchers wearing white lab coats. In another version of the study, the subject teacher conducted the experiment next to a confederate teacher, who was ostensibly conducting a similar experiment in view of the subject teacher. When the confederate teacher stopped the study at 330 volts, 90 percent of subject teachers would also stop the study.

What this indicates is that when modeling is present or when we are specifically called to act, going against the grain becomes significantly easier. The situational forces change. Doing what is right is easy when we are given indirect permission to act. *What is extremely difficult, however, is acting on our own without this indirect permission.*

We may not know exactly why the 10 percent act, but we do know what is different in the 10 percent. For whatever reason, their radars diverge from those of the other 90 percent of us. Their radars blink when the rest of ours remain silent.

What causes these 10 percent to have enhanced radars?

CHAPTER 6

Enhanced Radars: Awareness

THESE STUDIES REFLECT what most of us probably know intuitively: some people step up when the situation requires it, but very few people.

This phenomenon continues to be studied extensively. We don't have definitive answers about the 10 percent and what causes them to act differently, but we do know a few things:

- The 10 percent have enhanced radars—or, as I will call it, a *higher level of awareness*. This is reflected by the fact that 90 percent of people will act as the 10 percent did when the right thing is put on their radars by someone else (i.e., calling out to a stranger for help or stopping the shocks after seeing another do it).
- Going against the flow (i.e., culture)—or, as I will call it, *the default*—is extremely difficult, to the extent that 90 percent of us will not do it.
- The more we recognize the difficulty of going against the default, the more likely we are to do so.

- Most of us think we would act as the 10 percent do: help out the stranger or stop the shocks. Most of us, however, do not know ourselves very well. Ironically, it is likely the 90 percent (the ones who won't act) who think they are, in fact, the 10 percent. Thinking you would be part of the 10 percent is a strong indicator that you would be part of the 90 percent; that you don't question makes you more likely to flow with the default.
- The 10 percent were not necessarily born that way. Personality studies conducted on the 10 percent have consistently shown they are within the normal range, with nothing suggesting that they were born qualitatively different from the 90 percent.

It appears the 10 percent act from a different level of being than the 90 percent. If you ask them, they will say they don't know why they stepped up, they just did. There is something in their being that makes their radars blink when the radars of 90 percent of us remain silent.

Let's see if we can look behind the curtain of the 10 percent to see how they are made. Before we do so, I want to point out interesting results from behavioral brain scan studies to support the proposition that these people are indeed "made" and that we have the ability to increase our awareness.

According to Stanford neurobehaviorist Robert Sapolsky in his book *Behave: The Biology of Humans at Our Best and Worst,* studies have been conducted of people lying while undergoing brain scans. The brain scans invariably show that when people lie, certain areas of the brain light up or work harder. They do this to account for incongruity in perception—the mental effort it takes to lie and cheat.

In these studies, there were always a certain few (we know the percentage!) who did not lie or cheat. The question was posed whether this was the result of willpower or inherent nature. The brain scans of these people were then analyzed to determine the answer.

Their scans showed that the areas that typically lit up to indicate lying remained dormant. These areas of the brain in the nonlying few were not working harder. This reflected that their honesty was not the result of willpower but rather came naturally to them.

If they are not born this way and it is not the result of willpower, what is it that makes them different?

CHAPTER 7

Purpose

As the biologist said to the philosopher, "Shut the f—— up and make me my coffee." Too often we view philosophy as the hobby of intellectuals with no practical or real-world effect. If you are in that camp, I ask you to think about this issue every night or every morning. Pick a time and remain consistent—when you are brushing your teeth, when you are in the shower, or when you are driving to work. Think about it, think about it, and think about it. There is no more important ingredient in the creation of you than continually asking yourself, *What is my purpose for being here?*

This is your personal mission statement. Your answer to that question will likely change over time as you do. But do not let go of the reins. The power of you lies in that question and answering it for yourself. It is the source of your power. The power that will create you. A power that each of us has in equal degrees, separated only by who is giving it away to others. And most of us (90 percent) are giving it away without even realizing it.

CHAPTER 8

Creating Us

THERE ARE ONLY two things we *must* do in life: decide and die.

It is impossible for every one of us to not die. It is also impossible for every one of us to not decide. Everything else in life is optional; we have the choice whether or not to do it. For death and deciding, however, we have no choice. To not decide is to decide. Decision-making is built into the human process. It is forced upon us whether we like it or not.

Decisions are our tools. They are what create who we become. Each of us, to a certain extent, is the product of our decisions. With each and every decision, we are re-creating ourselves—constantly changing and constantly evolving through our decisions.

Some of our decisions are made consciously, but many of our decisions are made unconsciously. Those decisions emanate from somewhere. There is a source that directs them. That source is our personal mission statement: *What is my purpose for being here?*

That's a difficult question, and one that has generated and continues to generate an infinite number of answers. It takes energy and effort to answer that question. And when we do answer it, there always seem to be other equally valid answers. It's not only exhausting but also impossible to make money in trying to answer that question—those who do often go the way of the barista.

But when we don't answer that question for ourselves, we automatically accept as our answer what others have decided. Our source of decision-making in turn *defaults* to the answers of others. And when we default to the answers of others, we give away our power. We let others be the source of our decisions and, in turn, the source of our creation.

But when we answer that question for ourselves, we retain the source of our power. We are the ones directing our conscious and unconscious decisions, and we are purposefully creating who we become.

While this sounds like common sense, keeping our power is extremely hard. Ninety percent of us don't. Too many others are trying to take it from us as it becomes the source of their power—in fact, the success of many others depends on taking away our power.

It is arguably the hardest and most important thing you will do in your life, and yet, if you are like most of us, you won't.

Part 3

Decision-Making, Defaults, and Growth

Chapter 9

Defaults, Society's Default, and Other Defaults

THERE IS NO option—life requires that we answer its inherent question. It is fundamental in the decision-making process because we were created that way. And because we are born not to know, the question is by its nature subjective, and others profess to have clear answers for us, it's easy to default to the answers of others and let their default become ours. Others claim to know and at times do so resoundingly, so we think we might as well trust them. Or we don't even engage in the process of asking the question and in turn accept society's default answer as our own.

Society's default answer is symbolized:

Society's Default

Society's direction is summed up by Spock's words, "Live long and prosper."

Unless we decide for ourselves, we will likely default to Spock in our decision-making. Our decisions and life direction will be fostered by and default to society's directive to live long and prosper.

That will become our purpose. That will become our goal. That will become our destination.

Marketers know this all too well. We are bombarded with marketing encouraging us to buy a product to help us live a long time and maximize our prosperity: "If you sign up for our class, buy our product, or try our approach, your health and longevity will be improved, you will earn more money, have a more luxurious lifestyle, and enjoy more comfort."

Anyone who has children knows this, especially in the case of the first child: "These diapers are simply the best, you will not be a good parent unless you buy these diapers," or "If you want your kid to succeed, this baby formula is like no other for brain development."

Society's directive of living long and prospering is also why we become troubled when life events impede those directives. We cry injustice in the face of many common life events, often because they conflict with those two directives.

- Johnny got cancer at age thirty-two; life is so cruel.
- I worked so hard on that project, and it got a bad review. Life is just not fair.

- She exercised and ate well and died at forty-five. Life is punishing.
- That poor kid was born into a family of twelve kids with parents who are drug addicts. Life is harsh.
- That person was born on third base and thought she hit a triple. Whatever, she was just born lucky.

Injustice, unfairness, distress, and trouble are often the result of life events interfering with society's directive—to live long and prosper.

Society's answer is neither right nor wrong. It is simply an answer. A purpose. A destination for our decision-making. It is an option that we may choose to follow or not.

Other Defaults

Society provides the grand default of live long and prosper. That is likely the default for those who don't ask the question. For those who do ask the question but don't answer it for themselves, their answers will likely default to the answers given by:

- Genetics
- Parents
- Teachers and leaders
- Strong personalities, friends, and groups
- Religion and political parties
- Marketing and teams
- Self-created defaults

CHAPTER 10

Genetics and Parents

Genetics

THOMAS JEFFERSON PROCLAIMED in the Declaration of Independence that all men are created equal. While that may be true in terms of certain expectations we have of each other, we are not all created genetically equal. Some of us are born with more or less intellect, physical attributes, resources, and potential. We do not all start at the same point with the same resources.

We are all born with different gravitational fields—different genetic defaults. We share the same physical world, but we each exist in our own separate default worlds of creative potential. These default worlds create our gravitation fields for potentiality of direction, but, as we know from the social scientists, there is always the opportunity to break free into new and different worlds.

We have a son who was born with cognitive challenges. When he turned four, after speaking with an array of doctors and educational professionals, we brought him to see a neuro-psychologist. After a morning of testing, she met with us to discuss the results. She said he was two standard deviations behind the mean, about two years from his peers, and that about 85 percent of the time this gap increases with age. Fifteen percent of similar kids, however, are able to close the gap.

"Wow," my wife and I exclaimed. "How do they do that? How do they close the gap?"

The neuropsychologist said, "I don't know. Throw the kitchen sink at it."

She also said something that I will never forget and that my wife and I carry with us as it is simple, common sense, and yet profound for our gravity—our personal culture. After we were struggling to digest what she said, she continued, "I never said he will have a less fulfilling life; it will just be more challenging."

To put it another way, he has a different gravitational field than others—no big deal. He is simply creating himself in a different environment with a different field of potentiality.

His gravity remains strong. He needs to work significantly harder than others at just about everything. In some ways, his gravity prevails and the challenges mount, but in many ways, he is defying gravity and flying into a new world. He has a heart like no other. His unique default seems to allow him to connect to other unique defaults in special ways, allowing those around him to see life through a different set of eyes. It is our awareness of his genetic default that helped us push against it but also embrace the default world into which he was born.

Parents

Defaults are ingrained in us from birth through genetics. Our next set of defaults arises from our parents' belief systems, which automatically become ours, until we decide they shouldn't. We are brought up with religious, cultural, political, and ideological paradigms taught to or modeled for us. They create the gravitational field/culture in which we develop. They are the underlying framework through which we initially make decisions.

We are all raised with different belief systems, most of which are thrust upon us. And these thrust-upon defaults are not benign. Some children are raised to believe that those of different ethnicities, races, religions, or cultures are inherently less or more than they are. Often these beliefs are handed down indirectly, or even directly, through parents by their parents. They are passively picked up by children. These beliefs become the culture within which we develop.

In a well-known study, as reviewed by Zimbardo in *The Lucifer Effect*, Jane Elliott, a rural schoolteacher in Riceville, Iowa, developed an experiment that inadvertently demonstrated this effect—how easy it is to transmit belief systems/culture and how difficult it is to break this process. She devised an experiment to teach her students about prejudice and tolerance for diversity. The experiment hit home more than she or anyone could have predicted and has become widely cited in the social psychology field.

In her classroom experiment, Elliott arbitrarily designated one part of her class as inferior and another part as superior through the use of eye color. She told the students with blue eyes they were superior to those with brown eyes; she pointed to a variety of apparent supporting evidence for this theory, such as George Washington having blue eyes and a misbehaving child in the class having brown eyes. The blue-eyed students were told they were more intelligent and were given special privileges. The brown-eyed children were singled out as inferior and had to wear special collars to show their status.

Shortly after the experiment began, the blue-eyed kids refused to play with their brown-eyed friends and even instructed the school monitors that they should watch the brown-eyed kids for misbehavior. Fights soon erupted between the blue- and brown-eyed students. One brown-eyed boy proclaimed he punched a blue-eyed student because he had called him "brown eyes." Within a day, the brown-eyed kids began to do more poorly in their work and described themselves as sad, bad, stupid, and mean. Within a day.

The next day, however, everything changed. Elliott flipped the switch. She instructed the class that she was very sorry, but she had gotten it wrong. She had made a huge mistake. The research actually showed it was the brown-eyed kids who were superior; blue-eyed kids were the inferior ones. And sure enough, the kids were all too eager to switch roles. Rather than being sympathetic to their blue-eyed peers, the previously inferior brown-eyed students now enjoyed their status as the superior group and exhibited the traits of the previously superior blue-eyed kids. The brown-eyed kids now became the aggressive bullies. And the blue-eyed kids now became the victims, labeling themselves as bad and stupid.

These kids were told a story and let it govern their decision-making process without question. It became their culture. Their decision-making quickly defaulted to a new paradigm that in turn re-created them, for better or worse.

In another study reviewed by Zimbardo in *The Lucifer Effect*, a University of Hawaii professor conducted an experiment about our willingness to blindly act. He told his students that they were selected, based on their intellect, values, and education, to participate in an important university study. It was a study on how to control the population problem that was threatening the nation's security. He presented the students with evidence that had been gathered to show that mentally and emotionally unfit people were causing a drain on society's resources that would ultimately cause society to implode. He presented ostensible evidence to back up this claim, such as the use of resources for those who cannot sufficiently help themselves. He explained that the study was still in its infancy and no actions were imminent, but the students' intellect and opinions were needed to help with the study's design. He presented the students with a survey of seven questions that they collectively answered.

After the study was completed, the answers turned out to be relatively uniform and quite shocking.

- First, and not surprisingly, 90 percent of the students agreed that some people will always be more fit for survival than others.
- Second, 79 percent wanted one person to be responsible for the killing and another person to carry out the task.
- Third, 64 percent wanted anonymity for the person doing the killing.
- Fourth, 89 percent said painless drugs would be the most humane way to induce death.
- Fifth, 89 percent said they preferred to be involved in the decision to kill while only 9 percent wanted to be involved in the actual act.

- Sixth, 91 percent said that under extreme circumstances it was acceptable to eliminate those most dangerous to society, and 29 percent supported such action even if it had to be applied to their own families.
- And finally, and most shockingly, *only 6 percent of the students refused to answer the questions.*

Defaults and hence culture are easy to create for those in power. Parents start off with the ultimate power of a captive audience. Most parenting is done with good intentions, both for the children and for society. Rarely does a parent choose to instill anything other than what they believe to be the best for their children. Often parents purposely instill values that they hope will inform their children's decision-making and self-creation. And in hindsight, many of those values are a good thing, as they provide a foundational base.

As all of us were children, awareness of our parental defaults may help guide our decision-making as we move out into the world to self-create. We may agree with our parental defaults; we may disagree. Unless we are aware of their impact on us, they will likely covertly govern our decision-making and in turn our self-creation.

CHAPTER 11

Teachers and Leaders

Teachers

EDUCATORS ARE IN a profound position to direct the life purposes of their students through teaching, method, and environment. The educational environment both directly and indirectly establishes defaults in us.

My wife and I chose a family model of elementary school for our children. It was called *continuous progress*—one set of teachers and the same students remained in the same classroom environment from grades one through five. The model was based on family-style learning, where the students and teachers worked in close proximity and within a closed environment to guide each other.

The closed environment, duration, and intensity of interaction with the same group of students and teachers for five years provided a rich environment to set defaults. The intention was that those defaults would be uplifting and help positively guide the path for future decision-making and self-creation.

Defaults and culture were created: students were provided with a sense of empathy, compassion, giving, caring, and togetherness. As with any closed environment, some students were labeled as good, some as bad, some as popular, and some as looking to do anything to fit in. Their classmates were their family, and they were jockeying for position.

This model worked well for some and not so well for others. Most of the outcomes were based on how well the students fit in with peers and where they saw their standing within the small, closed community. One of our children struggled to fit in with peers during that five-year period and was at times excluded from social functions, labeled as the bad apple by other parents, and taken to task by teachers. None of this was intentional or unusual, but the length, intensity, and closed nature of the educational environment provided an atmosphere for defaults to become firmly rooted.

Our daughter never developed a sense of self or standing within this setting, and as she progressed out of this environment, she developed a default of low self-worth and not fitting in. As she now struggles with depression and poor self-image, we look to therapy to rebuild and reestablish her sense of self. She is fighting a firmly entrenched default, and it is proving to be an exceptionally difficult task.

Defaults and culture are rarely established with bad intentions, if they carry any intentionality at all, but awareness of their impact on our decision-making and self-creation will play a significant role in purposeful re-creation moving forward.

Leaders

Leaders exist to provide direction. They are our purpose helpers or our power takers, depending on the awareness of the interaction.

Many leaders bear similar qualities: definitive resolve, resolute answers, and a firm direction. They provide answers to life's inherent question. That question is hard by its very nature; there is no universally accepted answer. We are all left to our own devices. It takes a lot of work and effort to engage in the process of answering that question.

Often it is easier and safer to let others answer it and follow their lead. There are as many different leaders as there are answers. Often the stronger the leader, the more definitive they are in their answers.

The answers are unimportant. There will always be answers—new, different, and evolving answers. They are out there for our taking. What is important?

Awareness. If we willingly accept the answers of others, we are in turn giving them our power. We are hitching our creation wagon to their train. Our creation will evolve at the rate and to the extent they do. This is neither good nor bad, but it is a consequence. We all hitch our wagons to each other at different times. What is important is awareness—awareness of the hitching. Without awareness, we may remain blindly hitched when it's time to unhitch and find a new answer.

We are all leaders and followers of each other to some extent, and that in turn creates our culture. How aware are we of the power we are giving and taking from each other? If we assist others in answering questions for themselves, two radars have the potential for expansion. If we direct our answers at them, one radar remains stagnant for two people.

CHAPTER 12

Strong Personalities, Friends, and Groups

Strong Personalities

Strong personalities can be like magnets. People are attracted to their firm resolve and look to them for answers to life's question. That we are attracted to people with strong personalities and strong resolve may tell us about our own resolve.

Are we avoiding answering life's question for ourselves and looking to the strong personality for the answer?

Purposeful creation is not easy. There are strong magnets seeking to direct us. Are we aware of their pull?

Friends

Buddha was quoted as saying, "If it is purposeful change you seek, there is no more important ingredient than the company you seek."

Well before the field of psychology took hold, Buddha proclaimed what the social psychologists experimentally found to be true: decisions are significantly influenced by those around us by a factor of nine.

Ninety percent of the time we let others direct what is placed on our radars. Recall that 10 percent of the time volunteer teachers went to 330 volts when directed by the researcher in a white lab coat to do so. But when a peer volunteer teacher stopped before 330 volts, so did the subject teacher—90 percent of the time. Recall also that 10 percent of the time a stranger in a group setting, on his or her own accord, stopped to help a victim. But when the victim specifically asked the stranger for help, the stranger did so 90 percent of the time.

The power of gravity/culture on our decision-making process is influenced by a factor of nine by those around us. Our decision-making is easy or hard based on our acquaintances. As we will discuss in the next chapter, this factor of nine has been reinforced through brain scan studies that have shown we make emotional decisions ten times faster than logical decisions. When in group situations, we often act before we think. The group default and culture kick in. Gravity usually prevails. Why make it hard on ourselves to fight culture on a daily basis by surrounding ourselves with those whose answers are not what we desire for ourselves?

Groups

Humans are social creatures. Brain research has shown we are to a certain extent wired for social interaction. The pleasure centers of our brains activate through social connectivity. We derive comfort, safety, strength, and understanding through groups. Evolution has rewarded a pack mentality, and our brains have been wired accordingly.

Wiring for group inclusion, however, also results in the consequence of group exclusion—the us-versus-them mentality.

Grouping is a very powerful innate response within us. The brain makes distinctions between "us" and "them" almost instantaneously, well before that distinction can rise to the level of awareness. For example, as Sapolsky explains in *Behave* in functional MRI studies involving brain activity and decision-making, it was observed that the fear centers of our brains react to the face of someone of another race, gender, or social status in about fifty milliseconds. It takes the brain about five hundred milliseconds to be consciously aware of such differences. Innate grouping precedes conscious awareness of the grouping by a factor of ten.

Grouping is hardwired within us, and we have significant in-group biases whether we like it or not. We share positive emotional associations with people who share traits similar with us—values, beliefs, attributes, ideologies—and innately react accordingly.

For example, as Sapolsky states elsewhere in his text, studies have shown that when a victim is viewed as an *us* rather than a *them*, the odds of intervention are higher:

- Fans at a soccer match were more likely to aid an injured spectator if he was wearing the colors of the home team.
- When a stamped questionnaire was left on the ground near a mailbox, people were more likely to mail the questionnaire if it indicated support for their group's values.

According to Sapolsky, the pleasure center of people's brains activates equally whether their team wins or their rival team loses.

Often the goal of the *us* group is not to do well but to do better than the *them* group.

We view *them* as threatening, angry, untrustworthy, simple, and interchangeable. We view *us* as noble, loyal, and individualistic. It is an emotional response that requires less mental energy than rational thought. The response that requires the least mental energy, the default, usually prevails.

Grouping, like other defaults, is neither good nor bad. It is an innate part of human nature that helps us become who we are by aiding us in answering life's inherent question. But like other defaults, it is not without consequence. Grouping leads to emotional, innate decision-making favoring the in-group. This decision-making in turn innately creates who we become by default (i.e., without purpose) and sets the culture in which we create.

Awareness of the propensity for group default decision-making allows us to take purpose back. Recognizing that we are prone to making emotional decisions based on group biases allows us to slow down and let reason catch up to emotion, to fill the ten-to-one emotional responsiveness gap.

CHAPTER 13

Religion and Political Parties

Religion

OUR AWARENESS OF life's required question has led to the creation of a group whose primary purpose is to answer that question. Many of us look to religion as our source for the answer. We study the Bible, Quran, Shruti, and other religious books looking for direction. We look to religion for answers, and religions oblige us with directive—many in the form of answer books.

We give our power to religions to guide our creation. But how much purpose goes into that decision? Do we consciously choose the religious group to which we entrust our power?

Many of us set up study groups to review the guiding texts (i.e., the Bible or Quran) to assist in our decision-making process. Are we at times putting the cart before the horse? What about groups to discuss and consider the source of our guidance:

- How was the Bible derived?
- How was the Quran derived?
- Is this the source I want guiding me?

- Have I considered the variety of options?
- Or am I taking the source through default?

As religion has been established for the purpose of assisting with life's mandatory question, its role in our self-creation is enormous.

I was raised Catholic. I went to a Catholic school. I learned the rules and was scared to death of going to hell. I made sure I went to church every week and followed the prescriptive formula. In college, when my friends were home recovering from the previous Saturday night, I was at church making sure I was dotting my i's and crossing my t's. I was going to do what I needed to do to overcome the uncertainty of death and life. I was taught the formula and was going to stick to it. I knew the answers.

Then I went to law school and started to think about what I read and said. At church, I started to think about what we were mechanically proclaiming. A lot of it didn't make sense to me. A lot of it was inconsistent. I was basing my life on a formula that didn't seem right to me. It bothered me but not enough to do anything about it. I mean, what was I going to do? Who am I to question a historical institution? They knew better than I.

But a seed of doubt was planted. The inconsistencies of the answers kept bugging me, until finally I could no longer sit back and do nothing. I dug in with a passion. I looked into different philosophies and religions. But still who was I to question?

So I did what most people do (or maybe not): I quit my job, sold my house, and moved to California to attend Divinity School and further explore the groups set up to guide our answers to life's mandatory question.

It took me twenty years to finally free myself from my

Catholic default to the point where I can say I have my power back. There are many of the Catholic Church's answers that I agree with and use to guide my decision-making. But now I am purposely deciding which answers I agree with and which I do not. I am no more right or wrong than the church; I am just aware of what I am accepting as my answers for the creation of me.

Political Parties

Political parties have arisen because we have realized that consolidated power is more effective in directing society. Banding together for a cause has proven to be highly effective. "We are stronger together."

This strategy has proven to be highly effective and efficient in achieving certain societal results or goals. If we feel that certain results and goals are important, we join up in pursuit of those goals.

Fundamental life questions often become the platform for political parties: the right to life, the right to choose, the right to bear arms, and so on. We align with those who share similar values. We establish an "us."

The "us" then often drives the truck to which we hitch our wagon. We accept the group's collective decisions as our own, and we evolve as the group evolves. The party to which we attach will establish our gravitational field—our culture.

Awareness gives us three options:

- Hitch to the party and allow it to guide our creation.
- Hitch to the party and fight its gravitational field.
- Unhitch and purposefully decide if and when you will join up.

CHAPTER 14

Marketing and Teams

Marketing

TEN YEARS AGO my wife and I were approached at Costco by a team member who was looking to sell us the new membership card. She said, "For an extra fifty dollars a year, you will get 2 percent back on all of your purchases, and if at the end of the year the 2 percent does not equate to fifty dollars, we will send you a check for the difference."

I thought to myself, *Why would Costco go to the trouble of doing this? Seems like a no-lose situation for me. All upside and no downside. A lot of administrative burden for Costco.*

That was before I was aware of the power of the default and culture. Costco's program, like other loyalty programs, is looking to set our default. Costco will become your group; it will set the gravity for your shopping because you feel an attachment, an "usness" with them. Your first emotional decision will be to go to Costco. And as we learned from brain scans that reacted to pictures of in-group and out-group members, we make emotional decisions ten times faster than rational decisions. Once the default is set, we will react emotively 90 percent of the time.

I couldn't have been more wrong. No-lose proposition for me? More like a no-lose proposition for Costco.

How about credit cards? A few years ago I asked a fellow swim parent how much she paid for her hotel room. She said it had been free. "I signed up for the Marriott credit card. I got the equivalent of eight free stays just for signing up, and we get one free stay a year for the annual membership fee."

Wow, I thought. *No-lose situation*. I have not stayed at a non-Marriott hotel since that day. I guess I fit into the emotional 90 percent club.

Teams

I was a sophomore in college in September 1987 when ESPN's *SportsCenter* announced that the Minnesota Twins had clinched the division title and would be in the playoffs for the first time in my life. My roommates and I lived on campus in Wisconsin, where apartments were full of Minnesotans. The windows to our apartment were open; at the moment of ESPN's announcement, cheers erupted for no less than five minutes and could be heard all the way down the block. A feeling of euphoria had erupted like never before.

Professional sports provide a sense of unity and bonding that few other things do. As the 1987 Divisional Playoff Series unfolded, strangers with Minnesota Twins gear instantly became friends. The Twins won the World Series that year. It was the first professional sports victory for the state of Minnesota in almost all of our (the college students') lifetimes. There was nothing like it. We were together, and we were on top.

It's hard to pinpoint why. We were not on the team. We

did not do anything to cause them to win. Some of us didn't even follow baseball until that ESPN announcement. But it was "our" team, and we were better than every one of "their" teams. We were riding an emotional high, and there didn't need to be any rational reason for it.

We now know that "usness" is hardwired into our brains, and events that reinforce the specialness of us trigger our brain's emotional reward systems. That emotional feeling of "specialness," no matter how illogical, is powerful stuff and highly coveted. We want good feelings. We don't need rational reasons. We want feelings.

Many years ago I was chatting with a coworker about professional athletes and the athletes' accountability to the community for their actions. His response was, "They don't owe anything to the fans—it's just a business, and like any other business, the fans can choose to buy or not buy the product."

That's a very logical and rational response. But it ignores the "usness" that professional sports bring to the fans. There is an emotional feeling that is generated by our togetherness, especially when it causes us to be "special." It is not logical, but it is real.

As I was writing this section, my wife, my son, and I decided to go pick up dinner at the store. In the midst of getting our food, my son noticed a man with Down syndrome decked out head to toe in Green Bay Packers clothing. My son went up to him and gave him knuckles. We got to talking, and I asked the man if he was a Packers fan. His sister, who was with him, said, "Is he a Packers fan? You will never see him in any other clothes."

I then said, "Please tell me you were not born in Minnesota!"

His sister smiled. "He was a Vikings fan until the early eighties, when Tommy Kramer blew a game. He took the picture of Tommy Kramer, slammed it to the ground, and has never been a Vikings fan since that time."

Just then the man in the Packers outfit threw his hands downward as if smashing a picture to the ground. His sister then continued, "The following week he went to our sister's house in California, and the Packers were playing. They are a family of lifelong Packers fans. The Packers won that day, and they all went crazy. Since that day he has been Packers all the way."

I left the store thinking, *Professional sports really does bring people together to a greater extent than almost anything else. Total strangers talking and bonding over something they had no part in and that is absolutely inconsequential to their rational lives. It makes no logical sense. But it is undeniably true.*

Just as sports brings *us* together through emotion, it also provokes us to react emotionally against *them* when things don't go our way. The examples are numerous:

- A father sticking his finger down his throat and projectile vomiting over an off-duty officer and his daughter at a game in which his team lost
- Andrés Escobar murdered by a fan in Colombia two weeks after he accidentally scored a goal against his home team in a World Cup match
- An Iraqi soccer player shot by a fan of the opposing team as he was about to take a penalty kick

- Fans of the Vancouver Canucks destroying their town through riots after they lost game seven of the Stanley Cup finals

There are undeniably enormous emotional benefits associated with the usness of professional sports. We can have the experience of emotional togetherness along with behavior we are proud of through awareness—awareness that we are hardwired so our first experience in the moment will be emotional while it takes the rational brain time to catch up. With this awareness, we can hopefully catch ourselves making innate decisions in the heat of the moment that we may later regret while still enjoying the feeling of togetherness.

CHAPTER 15

Self-Created Defaults

Our Daughter

SOME DEFAULTS ARE bestowed upon us: genetics, parental legacy, and the early educational years. And some defaults are laid out by others for us to choose or join. But there is another category of defaults that gradually sneaks up on us—self-created defaults.

Our daughter has struggled with anxiety and depression since the age of thirteen. For months, she complained of middle school being a prison.

"I hate it so much," she would say. "Please, please don't make me go."

We struggled with what to do. So much conflicting advice from so many different people. Do we force her to go and send her to the lion's den? Or do we abide by her wishes and teach her to give up when times get tough?

We pushed her to go, but it was always with a compromise: "You can skip swimming if you go to school." "You can leave fifteen minutes early if you go today." "We'll take you out to dinner if…"

Soon the school was providing more and more accommodations: "You can eat lunch in the counselor's office so you don't have to eat in the lunchroom." "Teachers will give you a pass when you are anxious."

Each day the normal school routine slipped further and further away. We sent her to therapy. That helped at first, but soon it became less effective. One day, the Friday after Thanksgiving, she walked up to us and said, "Guys, I need help. I can't do this anymore. I need help. Take me to the doctor."

We called around, searching for options, and finally settled upon an "emotional support program" through one of the hospitals. Little did we know at the time that we were embarking on a long and difficult journey of setting a new default/culture for our daughter.

The program was comprised of struggling teens aiming to learn healthy emotional coping strategies. It also had a weekly meeting of the parents. Soon enough we realized what seemed like very odd behavior by our daughter was shared by many of the other kids. We took comfort in that.

You mean our daughter isn't the only one using social media like a diary and reaching out to kids she barely knows to share her mental health struggles? Well, maybe we're not the only bad parents in town.

That small comfort, however, was short lived. Soon our daughter started doing even stranger things: cutting her arms, not walking on cracks, refusing to use numerals in math.

Where is this coming from? we thought.

Just as we had felt an affinity with the parents, she had found an affinity with a set of friends to whom she could relate. Soon she was adopting their habits to fit in. The habits grew stranger and stranger and more and more intense. We were perplexed.

We went to different therapists; none of them had an

answer. Finally, I scheduled an appointment to see a psychiatrist at the Mayo Clinic. Within fifteen minutes of talking to our daughter, she was able to grasp what was occurring. I then chatted with the doctor, and she described all of my daughter's behaviors as if she had been living with us for the last year and a half. She said, "Look, this is going to be a long and difficult road for all of you. There are two things you must remember moving forward: Your first job is to keep her alive. And your second job, not far beyond the first, is to keep her out of the hospital."

I obviously understood job number one. But keep her out of the hospital?

"Don't hospitals make people better?" I asked.

She responded, "As you have seen, your daughter has such a poor sense of identity that she is like a magnet that picks up the personality traits of others. She feels a great affinity with others who are struggling and will pick up their habits. The hospital will reinforce this affinity, and she will be exposed to a significant number of unhealthy habits. Hospitals tend to be like revolving doors for these kids because they provide a comfort zone for them. They can avoid the social struggles of the real world by finding their way to the hospital."

She was Nostradamus that day. I found comfort in someone who understood what we were going through. I thought things would now start trending up, but they didn't. Our daughter continued to attend school and therapy programs. As the days went by, the school days grew shorter and the therapy days grew longer. We were struggling to get her to attend school, but she loved therapy.

At least we are keeping her out of the hospital, I thought. *We're struggling, but we're continuing to move past this, and she is not in the hospital.*

Then one day I got the call from the psychiatrist at her therapy program. After I returned from a series of meetings, I noticed four calls from the same number.

Oh no, I thought.

I called back, and sure enough it was the psychiatrist: "Your daughter is not safe to go home tonight. I'm sending her to the hospital."

"Please, please do not do so," I begged.

We talked, and finally she said, "If you don't give me permission, I'm going to send her involuntarily—"

"I have no choice?" I said.

She said, "No, not really."

She was sent to the hospital for a ten-day stay and has since been a revolving door over the last three years.

Her default was changed. The default for most teenagers is to get up, go to school, and engage in the routine, however difficult it may be. The more they do it, the easier it becomes. It becomes their mode of automatic action. Our daughter's automatic action in times of stress had changed to "going to the hospital." It grew so strong and intense that she continually found newer and more creative ways to get herself to the hospital: calling 911, calling suicide prevention, lying, falsely accusing, taking pills, driving to the hospital, all in an effort to get to the place of comfort—the hospital.

The hospital had become her default comfort zone, and changing it was like fighting gravity. "Not too far behind keeping her alive…keeping her out of the hospital. It will become her comfort zone, and it is very difficult to break."

We are still working to fight this gravity. Many times we are successful, but overcoming gravity requires constant propulsion until you reach the end of the atmosphere. If you let up, you will fall back.

Our Neighbor

I recently received an email from an old neighbor whom I had not seen in fifteen years: "Velner, your name came up in a conversation. Let's get together for coffee."

I loved him mostly because he and his wife were among the few people we knew who were honest and self-deprecating. Rather than starting a conversation with, "Just got back from my son's game; he's on the top team, and he's the top scorer," or "Just got back from the band concert where our son was first chair," or "I'll be late, I need to pick up our daughter from her gifted learning class," he reached out to me and said, "You'll appreciate this. You remember our daughter. You're probably not going to believe it, but she is an actual teacher, an actual teacher with a real job in a real town."

I just loved the honesty and openness. Yes, someone who was willing to show their flaws on their Christmas card. No need to put on the fancy clothes and fake smiles to tell everyone that you have checked all the boxes and have the white picket fence. True honesty and vulnerability. Our lives are not clean, easy, or neat, but they are our beautiful, messy lives. He didn't actually say that, but that was the gist of what I heard. And it was so refreshing.

We had coffee. I was on time, and he was about fifteen min-utes late. I sat there and thought, *Oh, f——. Here I was so refreshed by his vulnerability. I must have been wrong. What the heck? What an arrogant ass. Where is he? With all the shit I'm going through, I make an effort to be on time, and he is late. So much for his self-deprecation.*

He arrived and was very apologetic for being late. We made small talk for a while, and then he said, "Man, it's been a rough few years since I last saw you."

He filled me in on his kids and explained that he and his wife had just moved—downsized. We had about fifteen minutes of small talk, and then he said, "Man, life is tough. My mom died. My dad cheated on her…with another man. Can you believe that—with another man, at his age? He was in such rough shape after my mom died, I had to drop what I was doing and take care of him. It's enough to lead a guy to drink a little too much. And I drank a little too much. Almost destroyed my family. Can't believe my wife is still with me. She is a saint. But I'll tell you, thank God I found AA. Without it, I'd be dead. That's why I was late. I came from an AA meeting. I can't tell you, Velner, the urge to drink is so strong sometimes. I mean, it's like I'm fighting gravity. AA has saved me. It's spiritual; it's guidance to help me through this, support…"

He kept talking, but all I remember thinking was, *Did he just say it's like fighting gravity?*

Gravity, the same gravity that we were trying to overcome with our daughter, the unbelievably difficult gravity.

Did he really just say it's like fighting gravity?

So I asked him, "Did you just say, 'It's like fighting gravity'?"

He said, "Yeah, man, it's almost impossible. I can't do it alone. I need AA. I could not do it alone."

Wow, I thought. *He has created a new default for himself. And overcoming it is proving to be unbelievably difficult. Like 90 percent difficult. The same defaults that 90 percent of us do not overcome. The defaults that the social psychologists say are overcome by 10 percent of us.*

My neighbor and my daughter both are fighting against the 90 percent. It's the same thing—different only in form and appearance.

Then I got to thinking about AA and how he said it has saved him. I said, "Tell me a little about AA."

He said, "It's the only thing that can get me through this. It keeps me honest. It helps me understand that I have to keep pushing every day to get through this. And that I'm not alone."

I thought AA must be kind of like the confederate teacher in the lab or the victim specifically calling to the stranger. I thought, *Does AA expand his radar to foster awareness of things that are keeping him in his new default? Is AA inverting the nine-to-one ratio for him? Is AA the rocket fuel that fires continuously to get the rocket ship out of the atmosphere?*

We left the coffee shop, and I was grateful: honesty, vulnerability, and new awareness for me.

I went home and investigated the twelve steps of AA:

- **Honesty:** Fairness and straightforwardness of conduct; adherence to the facts
- **Hope:** To expect with desire; something on which hopes are centered
- **Faith:** Complete confidence; belief and trust
- **Courage:** Firmness of mind in the face of extreme difficulty; mental or moral strength to withstand fear

- **Integrity:** The quality or state of being complete or undivided; soundness
- **Willingness:** Prompt to act or respond; accepted and done of choice or without reluctance
- **Humility:** Not proud or haughty; not arrogant or assertive; a clear and concise understanding of what we are, followed by a sincere desire to become what we can be
- **Love:** Unselfish concern that freely accepts another in loyalty and seeks his good to hold dear
- **Discipline:** Training that corrects, molds, or perfects the mental faculties or moral character; to bring under control; to train or develop by instruction
- **Patience/Perseverance:** Steadfast despite opposition or adversity; able or willing to bear; to persist in an understanding in spite of counterinfluences
- **Awareness:** Alive and alert; vigilance in observing
- **Service:** Useful labor that does not produce a tangible commodity

There it was—twelve steps to overcome the gravity of substance abuse. But will this work for all of our defaults? Looking at the twelve steps through the purposeful decision-making lens, I summarized:

An awareness of the persistent need to earnestly, courageously, and honestly recognize and look beyond our defaults in a disciplined fashion toward the re-creation of our being, while humbly recognizing our (de)faults and troubles are not roadblocks toward the purpose of a tangible commodity but rather life planting seeds toward what we truly seek—growth.

Awareness, persistence…GROWTH.

Looking Back

As I get older, I often think about things in a new light, things that just seemed to "happen" but in hindsight were part of the 10 percent overcoming gravity. I recalled my time in high school when someone who later turned out to be a good friend of mine had just started hanging out with our group. I wasn't sure how or when he started hanging out with us, so I asked him, "How was it that we met? I recall that you used to always hang out with that different group."

He said, "I used to hang out with them, but I didn't like what they were doing or where they were going, so I tried to connect with Scott [an acquaintance of his who hung out in our group] to see if I could branch outside of my group. It kind of sucked, because I was an outsider for so long, and it's not like you warmly welcomed me."

I didn't really think anything of it, especially the "you not warmly welcoming me" part.

"Yeah, I kind of remember that," I said.

Now I realize how hard that must have been and the courage he had had to move on. The default would have been to stay with his current group. He fought that gravity and moved on. It could not have been easy. I'm sure he felt on many occasions that he was falling back toward Earth. It took awareness and persistence for him to branch out. But he was persistent, and eventually he broke out of his default atmosphere and into a new reality.

Awareness, courage, willingness, honesty, hope, perseverance, and patience. Not easy—but new realities await. The 10 percent exist many times right in front of our eyes, but they rarely hit our radars.

Right in Front of My Eyes

As I discussed above, our son was born with cognitive challenges. Almost everything he does is harder, including navigating social interaction and sports. He is the most social person I know. He needs social interaction like I need water. He craves it. He can be awkward with friends and sometimes gets excluded. He perseveres and keeps at it. He prods and probes with peers and seems to find his "right" level of interaction.

He loves sports, particularly basketball. He spends hours and hours in our driveway and garage practicing his shot and dribbling. He dribbles between his legs and works on his moves. He said to me this summer, "Dad, sign me up for traveling. I'm pretty good."

I said, "Bud, we might be moving too fast. How about house league?"

"No, that will be too easy for me," he said.

I said, "Let's try house, and then we can see if you want to do traveling next year."

He reluctantly agreed. There are tryouts for the house league—not for the purpose of cutting but to make sure the teams are even. Like any other hovering parent, I tried to stay and watch tryouts to make sure he was OK. No go. They kicked the parents out. "Sorry, folks, you can't watch. They'll be OK."

After tryouts were over, I was eager to hear how they went. "So, how'd it go, Bud?"

"It was OK."

"What do you mean? Some of those kids are pretty good, huh?"

He said quietly, "I'm about average."

All right, I thought. *This might be OK.*

He was placed on a team, fortunately, with two young adults as coaches. As I tend to hover, I watched all of his initial practices. After practice one day, I could sense they were all getting frustrated with him. I explained to the coaches that even though he had some developmental challenges, he absolutely loved basketball, that it meant the world to him. They were terrific. They spent extra time working with him and really appreciated his desire. How could you not? A kid with challenges and working hard. It doesn't get any better.

But for his peers, it can be irritating. He didn't really understand the rules, always asked to be passed to, and stood around half the time trying to follow the flow. They played him just the same as every other kid. He was out there moving and cheering on his teammates as they scored. Every basket was like winning the championship to him, and he cheered the others on as they scored.

His buddy was the most skilled player on the team. He scored half of the team's points every game. Shoot a three, drive to the hoop—he was out there doing it all.

But he was even more extraordinary in another respect. He was always looking to pass, especially to my son.

"Move, get open," he would say.

He looked to pass to my son almost as often as he looked to score. Others on the team grew frustrated with my son's friend, as many of the passes ended up becoming turnovers. That did not deter him, however. One time he finally found my son under the hoop alone, made a perfect pass and…there it was—my son's first basket.

My memory is probably a bit skewed at this point, but all I remember is the entire team jumping up and the bench running on the court to hug him. It was the middle of the game, but you would have thought they had just won in overtime. I was crying. So happy for him. I looked for his friend. He was not there in the group hugging him.

Man, where is he? I thought.

He was standing back from where he made the pass. He just looked at my son and pumped his fist.

I will never forget that basket, and I will never forget his friend. The default and culture for the team was to win and score. That typically didn't include involving our son on offense. But this friend's radar said otherwise.

It Doesn't Feel Right

As I look back on life, there are certain pivot points where one decision could have changed everything. One of those points for me was studying for first year, first semester finals in law school.

I never considered myself one of the smart ones. I wasn't dumb but was never seen as the smart kid.

Law school is unique. There are no tests until the final exams. An entire semester is graded according to one four-hour essay final for each class. Not only is the pressure intense, but there is also a ton of material that you must know and synthesize. Around Thanksgiving, classes wind down and students begin to study. Most students study in groups and prepare outlines for the exams.

You take one, I'll take another, and then we'll divvy up the work is often the standard course.

We were in a group of about four. We got together to talk about outlines and who was going to do what. For whatever reason, continuing with the group dynamic didn't feel right. I didn't feel like I was synthesizing the material the way I should because I wasn't working individually on each outline.

I said, "Guys, I'm going to study on my own for this. I'm going to make my own outlines for each class."

"Dude, what the hell. Are you sure? Do you know how much work that is?"

"Yeah, I don't know. It just seems like I'll synthesize the material better if I put in the work for the outline."

And so I did. I dug in for a week straight. I went at it morning, day, and night over the course of Thanksgiving week. The tests came. I was confident. I knew the material, and I was able to confidently organize it. I sat; I read; I organized; and I wrote. As the tests were all essays, there was really no way of knowing how you did. I thought I had done OK but wasn't really sure.

Hopefully well enough to keep going, I thought.

Six weeks later we all stopped by the office to get our grades. I picked up mine and waited until I got on the bus to look at the paper. When I did, I almost fainted: A, A, A, A, B, B.

Holy shit, I thought.

These must be someone else's grades. But there it was: my name on the top. About a week later they handed out class ranks. Law school is a small environment. Everybody knows everything about everybody else. There were perceptions about who the smart ones were. And this group certainly didn't include me or my group of friends. We were the typical partying college kids who were not on anyone's radar as smart.

I was in the library, and I remember overhearing, "We still don't know who is number one. It's not Jennifer, Rick, or Jay."

These three were all older students from the state legislature. I assumed, by default, like most of the other students, that for sure one of them would be number one.

Their conversation continued: "Are you sure it's not Jennifer?"

"Yes, I'm sure. I just asked her."

Later that day I stopped by the office to pick up my class rank. The administrator handed me a small sticky note folded over. I opened it. 1/103.

Never in a million years would I have thought this would be me. As it came time to study for finals, something in me said, *You need to go a different route.* I listened, and everything changed.

Constant Firing Is Required

I grew up in a household where my parents did not buy us any wants. If we wanted something, we needed to earn it and buy it for ourselves. At the time, I was always so mad. After hockey games, when other kids were walking up to their parents to get a quarter for a pop, mine would always say, "There's a drinking fountain right over there."

After a while, I stopped asking. I learned quickly that if I wanted a pop I would need to work and bring my own quarters. And so I did. I got a paper route in fifth grade, caddied all summer long, and my bank account grew. I bought myself my own waterbed, my own black-and-white TV, and my own three-in-one stereo in sixth grade. Pretty big deal back then.

I paid for my college and law school educations through loans and grants. I'm incredibly grateful for the default/culture of personal responsibility my parents set for me.

If you want something, it is up to you to go after it and get it.

It has served me well over the years. But it has also made me cheap. I still recall in college when I debated whether I wanted to spend one dollar on a pack of gum. My default is that one dollar is a lot of money, and it can sometimes be painful to part with.

It has taken me a long time to even become aware that I am cheap. But it's now on my radar, and it's difficult to overcome. I was recently out for dinner. I sat debating whether I would tip six dollars or eight dollars on a forty-dollar check. I settled on six dollars. As I walked out, I thought, *You ass, come on. Two bucks: it probably means so much more to that college kid working as a waitress than it does to you. You sit and debate over two bucks and then end up going the cheap route.*

It's still hard for me to part with two bucks. But I'm aware, and the engines are firing. I still fall back to Earth and hold on to the two bucks, but at least now I have to part with it more often. There may be a time after I fire long enough that I get beyond gravity and enter a new reality where giving away the extra two bucks becomes my new default.

Unlimited

We are born with some defaults, and others are bestowed upon us by our upbringing. But the majority of our defaults are self-created. We create our own defaults/culture by rigid thinking, repeated unconscious or semiconscious decisions, blind acceptance, fear, surrender, arrogance, ignorance, and laziness. Purposeful decision-making is hard. It requires effort and the courage to go it alone if need be.

All of us have created and will continue to create our own defaults. They will play a part in our decisions. And our decisions will play a part in who we become both individually and as a company.

Defaults and culture are the self-created status quo and wield power over us until we become aware of their existence. Without awareness, they will govern our creation.

Awareness means continually scanning for our defaults—fleshing them out, bringing them to the surface, and recognizing they play a part in our decision-making process.

CHAPTER 16

Defaults: Our Beautiful Messes

IT'S EASY TO think of our defaults as obstacles or faults to be overcome. They make life harder and more inconvenient. They get in the way of what we want and who we want to be. Often our default is thinking of our defaults as messy problems.

But without them we would have no home base from which to operate. They are the place from which we operate to self-create. They are our comfortable houses. They are always there for us as a safe haven, and we can stay there for as long as we desire. But invariably there comes a time when we need to leave home for bigger things. Comfort is no longer enough; we need to move on and grow. Something inside us says, *Time to move on. This default has served you well. You need to move on and work toward a new house, a different house.*

And then we move on from there. Once we become settled, we decide it is time to move on. But why do we do that? Why do we leave a perfectly good house for the possibility of a new one? There is no logic to this.

We do it instinctively. We yearn for and desire the possibility of something more at the risk of leaving the security of the existing. It is innately within us, the desire for growth.

But growth is difficult to see. It is the process that evolves while we are engaged in seeking a new destination. It is so simple on the one hand but on the other hand becomes so buried that it becomes obscure. We are bombarded every day with others telling us that the purpose is the destination:

- You're almost there. All you need to do is make another $10,000 per year.
- Just one more cute outfit should do it.
- Surely you'll be there if you reach number one in your law school class.
- The championship—that's it; if we win the championship, we will be at the pinnacle.
- I just need to be a little kinder and everything will be OK—volunteer a little more, donate a little more money because doing so will make someone out there live a little longer or prosper a little more.

But we do those things, and still we yearn for more: more clothes, more number ones, more championships, more giving, more prosperity for ourselves and others.

We go around and around.

Where is the finish line?

Almost there.

Almost there.

OK, I know—I'll just read this book. That's the answer. They have the formula. Hold on, let me read this book, and then everything will be different.

We have been searching for the ultimate destination forever. What was once so simple to see has become buried. We are in the middle of it and can't see it. We are searching for this place called Earth.

"Where is Earth?" we all ask.

I found it, hold on, just one more book.

All the while it's right under our feet. The Earth is growth. The Earth is the journey. It is so simple but so obscure. It is obscure because it gets buried while we seek the destination. As John Lennon said in the lyrics of "Beautiful Boy," "Life is what happens while we are planning for it."

CHAPTER 17

Growth

WE HAVE CHOICE in determining our purpose. We can choose the destination as our purpose. Destinations are places, events, objects, or results for which we strive but ultimately do not endure. They are temporary landing spots: longer lives, comfortable lives, promotions, bigger houses, more children, perfect children, the picket fence, the perfect Christmas card, the championship, the number-one class rank, the recognition, the legacy, the impact we have on another...

Destinations all have one thing in common: they are temporary. One day they will be gone. They have to be temporary because that is the fundamental nature of life. We were created with one and only one immutable element: change. It is the underlying, fundamental force of everything. It is the common-sense, simple element that triggers everything—one we often ignore because it gets buried.

The destination—the infinite number of possible destinations—is often the purpose that guides our decisions and governs our self-creation. Invariably, however, the destination never arrives, or when it does, it eventually fades away. It has to because that is the way the process was set up. All destinations change and eventually fade away. There is no other way.

Society tells us every day, every hour, every minute that the destination is the purpose. Destinations, however, are illusory purposes—illusory because they will ultimately fade away.

We have another option in choosing our purpose. This other option is awareness of that which at one time seemed simple and common sense: the purpose of change, the destination of growth. Change is the only consistent and enduring element of life, and growth is our strongest desire. Change and growth are the Earth that we don't see because we are standing on it. They are the processes that we don't see because we are engaged in them. They are life occurring while we are planning for it.

Chapter 18

When Messes Become Beautiful

W HEN GROWTH BECOMES the purpose, our messes become trans-formational. Messes are typically things that get in the way of our destination. My son was born with a cognitive challenge—*Oh man, how are we going to survive? Life is going to be so difficult. Why is life so unfair?*

Or *why did our daughter, and our family, get so unlucky to be stuck with mental illness—what did we do to deserve this?*

Or *I worked my butt off for that promotion, showed up every day… and yep, sure enough, sorry.*

Or *I was so kind to that person, gave her all my attention and time, and she continues to treat me like shit and wallow in her own misery; she is so ungrateful.*

Or *lung cancer at thirty-eight, and all he did was exercise and lead a healthy lifestyle. So unfair.*

We all die. It's part of the process. Just another element of change. We all set destinations that never arrive or do and then fade away. It's part of the process. Just another element of change. When our destinations get moved, rearranged, or destroyed, we call them messes. Yet these messes are ultimately catalysts for changing our perspective, seeing things differently, experiencing a new feeling, intensifying our feelings, arriving at a new understanding, taking an unexpected journey, and showing us new ways to color, cook, draw, sing, dance, write, and love. They are new and unexpected paints for our canvasses, tools for our sculptures, spices for our soups, and lyrics for our music. They are life's way of giving us what we never knew we needed or wanted.

I will never forget when the psychiatrist called me to say that she was sending our daughter to the hospital—the hospital we worked so hard to keep her out of. I thought over and over that day, *Our lives will never be the same.*

And I was right. I describe that day as a rocket ship arriving and transporting our family to a new reality. It is a reality that I never knew existed. A reality that I never would have chosen. But it is a reality where undoubtedly our family has grown in ways previously unimaginable. We do not look at life the same way. We feel more intensely. We love more deeply. We are more empathetic. We are more appreciative. And, sure, we are more tired.

The same applies to the situation of our son. I will never forget the day I drove home from a fishing trip to see my in-laws' car in the driveway. I immediately knew something was wrong. I walked in the door.

"Something is wrong with Vinny," my wife said. "He doesn't respond when called. He only hears things on occasion. The doctors think something is wrong."

We ultimately learned that he was born with cognitive

challenges, as I have explained. We thought, *Our lives will never be the same. This is not what we expected.*

And we were right. Our lives have changed in unimaginable ways. Unimaginable but unexpectedly beautiful—we were plunged into a new reality where we experience things in a simpler, cleaner, clearer way through him. We are able to feel true and deep love because he does. We are able to see how life can be when one doesn't care what others think. Because of him.

It is messy; it is hard; it is confusing; it is exhausting. But we are so grateful and fortunate. Our messes have been the catalysts for us to make a more flavorful life soup, a more colorful life painting, a more intense life song, a more intricate life dance (although I don't really dance).

CHAPTER 19

Doing versus Being

It is often asked what we can do to expand our radars.

> What can we do to be more aware?
>
> What can we do to be fulfilled?
>
> What can we do to be the one who steps up when the situation calls for it?
>
> What can we do to be part of the 10 percent?

As mentioned in the beginning of the book, brain scans of the 10 percent have revealed that their actions are not driven by willpower but by a different sense of being. The responses of the 10 percent after stepping up usually match this revelation: "I have no idea what caused me to do that. I just did. It was just a natural response. Nothing special I did. Just something inside of me."

Their being caused them to step up. They just reacted.

What can I do to be like that?

It is often said that you cannot do anything to change your being. Doing will never get you there. It will only keep you on the merry-go-round. It's about being. We are human beings, not human doings. I've heard that many, many times, often from someone trying to sound enlightened or wise. But what does that mean? It's a great sound bite. But seriously, let's get practical—how does that help me? We do. That's why we were created. If we didn't do, we would be plants, or trees, or grass, or rocks. We are humans. Doing is what we do.

A little social psychology, messy experience, and common sense to the rescue, maybe.

Let's reframe this to journey versus destination. We can put our arms around that. I often recall driving in our family van for spring break to Florida: thirty hours, six people, and a dog in the car for a two-day nonstop trip from Minneapolis to Fort Myers. All of us kids complained, "Why can't we be like everyone else and fly? We have to drive; what a waste of time. We just want to get there."

And now, all these years later, I don't recall much of Florida, but I do recall with fondness the drive, the stops along the way, the cribbage we played, the sleeping in close quarters, the dog licking our faces, the unique rest stops, the different cultures after crossing into the South, the "Hi, y'all." At the time, the journey was overlooked as a necessary evil to get "there." But in hindsight, the doing provided a destination for the journey, and it was the journey that really mattered.

When we "do," we are seeking a destination, a result, a Florida. It only makes sense: There must be a purpose in mind for our action. The underlying purpose that frames the decision that drives the creation.

We do to get "there." But the destination fades away. It is illusory, existing to provide the process. That's the merry-go-round:

striving and striving, doing and doing, searching for the magical place called Earth but never finding it. We are standing on it but never see it. It is life happening while we are planning for it. Doing is the planning for life, while life is what is occurring during the planning. We do and do and do to get there and there and there. But the ultimate "there" never comes.

So if doing will never get us there, then what?

How do we expand our radars?
How do we become more aware?
How do we expand our being?

That is where messes come in. Messes are the journey—the thirty-hour van trip to Florida that we never wanted to take but circumstances threw at us. Our life messes are opportunities for new experiences, to see things in new ways, to bring forth parts of ourselves in new creative ways.

Throughout all of our daughter's mental health struggles, my wife and I have at times been accused by various therapists of being responsible for her condition, for neglecting or abusing her. At first, we were irate. I mean, really irate: *What the…are you kidding me? They have no idea of our family history.*

Then we started to question ourselves. *Maybe we are not good parents. We did the best we could.*

Then we went through the process and finally regained our confidence. We have given everything to parenting and done our absolute best. And a part of us asks why. *Why is life throwing this mess at us? We've given everything to do the best we can as parents. We are so unfortunate. No one can understand what we are going through. Poor me.*

And then I recall what I've heard for years and years and at one time thought I understood but now know I did not remotely understand. On multiple occasions, through movies, the news, or conversations, I have heard people of color claim that others have no idea what it is to be judged for nothing they did: "White folks have no idea what it's like to walk down the street and have people move to the other side, clutch their purses a little tighter, or lock their car doors. In their minds, you are guilty until proven innocent—not because of anything you have done, but because of the color of your skin."

I always thought I understood what that meant. But I had no idea until having been falsely accused myself. I was so irate. Guilty until proven innocent.

I don't think anyone has any idea how horrible this is, I thought on multiple occasions. Until it finally hit me: *You don't think anyone has any idea? There are millions of people who have an idea; they live it every day. The only difference is now you have an idea of their existence. Wow*, I thought. *Kind of selfish of me.*

It took a while to really sink in. I was experiencing a bit of what others live through every day. I believe I now have a better idea of the different reality in which people of color exist, although I'll still really never know. This messy experience has caused me to experience a different reality that has helped me feel more intensely, be more empathetic, and see and experience things differently through a new lens, an expanded radar. I believe my being has been expanded through this mess—I mean opportunity. Not because of anything I did; doing was not involved. What was involved was recognition through experience—the journey bringing forth new, hidden elements within me. The journey expanding my being, expanding my radar, to continue my existence through an expanded "home base."

Every day we have messes in our lives. They usually arrive based on our defaults. They are different for each of us. They are our opportunities to expand our being. Not by doing but through a change in perspective. Rocket ships to take us to a new reality. Rocket ships to help evolve both our personal and company cultures.

Practical Tools for Company Risk Mitigation and Employee Radar Expansion

Purposeful decision-making and radar enhancement are nice concepts, but is there any practical impact to be derived from this understanding? How can we implement those concepts to promote cultural change within our organization and within ourselves?

Awareness of our tendency to sleepwalk and create by default is the first step. The next steps involve implementing measures to act on that awareness through promoting employee radar expansion to uncover the unknown unknowns and do the right thing.

The following are fourteen tools to guide companies to do the right thing through raising the unknown unknowns to awareness. Following the company tools are twelve tools to foster employee growth and radar expansion, as well as the personal benefits that follow.

CHAPTER 20

Company Tools to Uncover the Unknown Unknowns

1. Organizational Structures

RADAR EXPANSION AND cultural growth are difficult—very difficult. But there are tools that can make fleshing out the unknown unknowns easier. These tools act as agents sent out into the environment to dig up the unknown unknowns and plant seeds on employees' radars.

Most organizations have structured their processes so the default issues (process, profits, and succession) consistently remain on the company's radar. The CEO is the captain of the ship. What is on his or her radar will inevitably dictate the company's evolution. Who has discretion to place matters on the CEO's radar is often carefully orchestrated. The CFO is charged with making sure the profits are always on the CEO's radar. The COO is charged with making sure that process efficiency is always on the CEO's radar. And the quarterly and year-end reports are charged with keeping succession on the CEO's radar. These three defaults are the backbone of almost every company, and it's imperative for purposeful evolution that they consistently remain on the CEO's radar screen.

But what about DTRT? Where does that fit? Is there a separate company officer charged with keeping it on the CEO's radar? Often there is no one charged with DTRT, or it falls to the legal department—that same group of people who moonlight as baristas or debate over the definition of "is"! If the company does have a DTRT department, to whom is it reporting? Is the company structured so the DTRT officer has direct access to the CEO's radar screen? Or is the DTRT officer reporting up through a gatekeeper officer?

If those charged with DTRT do not have direct access to the CEO, there is a strong likelihood DTRT will get buried or simply become trite. DTRT does not provide immediate returns and is often overlooked as the more immediate default issues press for time. The CEO is charged with maintaining a long-term vision for the company and to do so effectively should have a wide and active radar screen.

If the DTRT officer needs to report up through a default officer whose radar screen is narrower (such as the CFO), DTRT is now fighting gravity. The CFO's primary charge is profits, and that sets the default gravity. If DTRT needs to make its way through the profit department to make it to the CEO, gravity suggests that it often will not. Making it past the CFO will require constant awareness, which we know from social psychologists is a difficult task. A task that 90 percent of the time will not happen.

Companies are often missing a radar helper to invert the nine-to-one ratio—the victim on the street specifically calling out or the coteacher modeling DTRT.

2. Culture

Structuring a company's processes to help keep DTRT on the CEO's radar is one step but a small one. Most decisions are made at the everyday, every-employee level that never make it to awareness. To counteract this lack of awareness, the company needs its agents to hit the environment and start digging. To be effective, DTRT needs to be an "all on board" process.

It starts with culture. That is another word that can become trite, spoken to pat ourselves on the back, a concept with no meat on its bones. To put meat on the cultural bones, culture needs to remain consistently active in a manner similar to what rituals do for individuals.

Rituals require eyesight and consistency, and so does culture. My current company has DTRT as its mission statement splashed all over the company's property—on common area walls, meeting room walls, company T-shirts, websites, and stationery. It is consistently talked about at meeting updates. Effort is made to keep it in eyesight and earshot as often as possible.

The company also rewards decisions that consider factors other than process, profits, and succession. By reward, I mean public acknowledgment for taking the time and energy to consider another's perspective. As we now know, it takes much more mental energy to consider the perspective of an "other," as the rational portions of the brain need to be activated. It is much easier to go with the emotional response of the default, the us mentality that activates the emotional parts of the brain to release our feel-good neurotransmitters. Comfort food is hard to pass up. My company recognizes this uphill battle and provides positive feedback for those putting in the extra effort.

During my twenty-five years as an attorney, I have seen many different styles of partnerships, as attorneys are often involved in documenting the up-front structure of the deal. I've also seen these partnerships break down, as I am involved in partnership disputes and litigation. I'm involved in the front end of partnerships, when everyone is singing "Kumbaya," and the back end of the partnerships, long after the guitars and singing have stopped.

One of the things I often say is you can have the best and most expensive documents in the world to keep the partnership in line (baristas are not cheap), but if you have a partner who is not DTRT-centered (who is committed to making decisions outside of the default), when issues arise (and they always do), there will be messy fights. DTRT in both members acts as a hot air balloon for the partnership, creating levity when the gravity of each company's default kicks in.

To keep the hot air firing, however, every company employee must recognize the importance of DTRT in every interaction, recognizing that it is not just some trite concept but the help necessary to rise up against our inherent gravity, recognizing that each employee is empowered to be the victim specifically calling out or the coteacher modeling DTRT. The goal is to keep employees aware of the concept of culture so DTRT starts to become the default and instinctively appears on their radars. And as it appears on more and more of the employees' radars, they begin to act as coteachers for each other, creating a cycle that keeps the hot air firing.

3. Getting to Know Each Other

Every one of us has a story. Each of us has unique life experiences. Each of us has unique job experiences. Every employee overcomes obstacles every day on the job. Life is messy, especially at work! These messes are best shared. Because with every mess, there is often a creative solution.

But sharing the messes and their solutions is hard because they are so voluminous that they rarely rise to awareness and often remain concealed within a single employee. Mess sharing doesn't come through formalized interaction, because often only the known knowns and known unknowns are discussed there. Mess sharing comes through informal interaction that generates dirt flying into the air by shooting the shit. We never know what seeds may later germinate by the sharing of our dirt, but we do know that germination has no chance if the dirt remains stuck.

My company, probably like many companies, offers lunch once every few months for the low price of engaging with someone you do not know. In a similar way, it has also structured random get-to-know-you lunches where names are randomly selected as lunch partners. These informal getting-to-know-you events are great agents for digging up the unknown unknowns. They operate to loosen the stuck dirt of our messes, cause the seeds to fly, and ripen our radars for germination.

The interesting thing about these low-priced lunches, however, is that relatively few people partake, and many who do don't hold up their end of the bargain by sitting with someone unknown. Getting to know an "other" is hard. It requires more mental energy to engage the rational parts of the brain associated with perspective taking. It's much easier to stay within our groups and enjoy the comfort food released by emotional neurotransmitters. Apparently free lunch is no match for the comfort food of these emotional transmitters.

But maybe it would be different if we recognized that there is personal benefit in it for us as employees. The personal benefit of radar expansion and purposeful growth. It is much like eating healthy or exercising. Hard to do initially, but we are often glad once we've done it.

Sometimes we need a push to exercise or eat healthy. Free lunches may just be that push.

4. Group Activities with Other Departments

Group activities operate in the same manner as lunches, allowing us to informally get to know one another and share our dirt. The key is engaging other departments so we can hear the stories of those different from us. Group activities provide grounds to informally realize there are many ways to think about issues that we have responded to in one particular way. Failure to experience how others act can lead to lone-wolf actions and often produce unintended consequences that only arise after it is too late.

That is what happened with the Abu Ghraib prison scandal described by Zimbardo in *The Lucifer Effect*. As the Iraqi war was winding down in the early 2000s, the United States needed a prison to house Iraqi detainees. Abu Ghraib had been an Iraqi prison in the center of Iraq, where it housed Iraq's most dangerous criminals. After Iraq was liberated, the United States decided it would use Abu Ghraib as its war prison.

War is a novel situation in which the army is often in reactionary mode. The United States needed someone to organize and run the prison under very chaotic and stressful conditions. The Abu Ghraib prison had become so dilapidated that it had no sanitary sewer system and no means by which to adequately segregate the expanding prisoner population. The US government originally tapped a high-ranking officer to oversee the refurbishment of Abu Ghraib, an officer who had little prior experience setting up or managing prison systems. Early on the officer was often absent, and the guards were left to their own devices to establish the prison protocol. No protocol was established, and the prison atmosphere was essentially mayhem, with prisoners unsegregated by age, gender, or mental condition and with Iraqi citizens having been hired as guards when at times they needed to be guarded themselves. The prison was in complete disarray, particularly Tier 1A, which was headed by a lower-level officer.

This Tier 1A officer was initially placed in charge of four hundred prisoners, but soon that number grew to one thousand. Among those one thousand were high-value ghost detainees. High-value detainees were considered open to all-means-necessary information extraction in which military intelligence officers out of uniform conducted extreme interrogation techniques. Unbeknownst to this Tier 1A officer, those techniques ended up being his default and created the culture by which he established his prison protocol.

This officer had almost no formal training for establishing the prison protocol: his training consisted merely of a one-hour cultural awareness class. He was essentially left to his own devices to figure out how to set up and run a prison unit. He had no coteacher to model the process for him other than the military intelligence officers softening up the high-value detainees. He also had no supervision or accountability because his supervisors had no experience in prison protocol. When he asked for support, his supervisors often responded that he should make do with what he had and see what he could come up with. When he requested assistance, he was chastised for complaining.

The prison operated in almost complete anonymity. With too much downtime, chaotic conditions, a lack of protocol, and modeling only of prisoner abuse by the military intelligence officers, the conditions soon devolved into total disarray. Prisoners were forced to wear women's panties on their heads;

prostitutes were housed with men and children; prisoners were forced into sexual stress positions; naked men were stacked in pyramids; soldiers stood with naked prisoners for trophy photos; prisoners were led around on dog leashes; male prisoners were forced to masturbate in front of the female guards; and hooded prisoners were forced to stand on boxes with wires attached to their extremities under the belief that if they fell they would be electrocuted. The prisoners were essentially treated as toys. This mentality spread to much of the guard staff, and soon the behavior became a game in which trophy photos and videos were taken and electronically circulated for the amusement of others. The gravity of the situation had taken on a life of its own until the radar screen of one low-level army employee started to blink.

One of the trophy video clips made its way to a soldier named Joe Darby. Darby was a twenty-four-year old army reservist (the lowest of ranks) who was initially amused at what he saw but later became more and more disturbed. He said that after receiving the video clip, he sat with the disturbance for three days and eventually decided to anonymously turn it over to military authorities because it violated everything he personally believed in. Darby was the lowest-ranking officer on his unit and risked significant repercussions for going against what had become a very strong default culture. Speaking up essentially meant alienating himself from his unit, his comrades—his peers.

After media reports started to surface the issue, the government initially responded that it was an isolated incident, the product of a few bad apples. General Myers (the highest officer in operational command) initially publicly commented that there was no evidence of systematic abuse, that 99.9 percent of the soldiers were behaving in admirable ways and DTRT.

By 2006, however, it surfaced that there were more than four hundred military investigations into similar abuse scenarios. The Abu Ghraib prison scandal has become the poster child of how situational forces and extreme cultures can overwhelm common sense and make it extraordinarily difficult to call out the gravity of a situation for what it is. Abu Ghraib has been routinely studied by social psychologists for what can happen when systems go unchecked, when we don't make sure that departments look after each other, when we don't establish protocols that encourage the stranger on the street to specifically call out or provide for modeling coteachers.

At Abu Ghraib, the gravity of the situation prevailed and was only brought to light because it hit the radar of one of the 10 percent (a low-level soldier who was personally disturbed by what he saw). The Abu Ghraib prison experience proved to be a real-life demonstration of what had been observed decades earlier in the laboratory of the Stanford Prison Experiment.

Designed by Zimbardo, the Stanford Prison Experiment was a mock prison scenario that investigated the effects of power and systems left unchecked. College-age students participated in a study designed to observe the effects of unchecked guard power on both guards and prisoners. The students were randomly selected as either guards or prisoners in what was to be a two-week experiment. The guard abuses, however, quickly overwhelmed all those involved, and the experiment was halted after only six days. The guards' relatively unchecked power almost immediately shut down their commonsense radars, and they began subjecting the students/prisoners to the same types of deprivation and humiliation revealed decades later, in real life, at Abu Ghraib—including forced sexual positions, forced stress positions, isolation, and extreme psychological gamesmanship.

The effects of the Stanford Prison Experiment and its real-life counterpart at Abu Ghraib have revealed that systems and behavior that create an us-versus-them mentality, when left unchecked, can quickly lead to a culture that creates forces in which common sense has almost no chance. These unchecked systems and behavior include:

- Seeing *them* as less than human
- Defused responsibility
- Anonymity
- Unchecked "groupthink," where dissent is suppressed, conformity is pressured, and counterinformation is withheld
- Lack of oversight by "outside forces"

Abu Ghraib is obviously an extreme example but illustrative of what can happen when the lone wolves are set to roam free. It is often easy for departments to operate in isolation (such as the department described in Part 1 of this book that was allowed to operate as an unchecked lone wolf due to strong profit generation despite the fraudulent accounts) so that groupthink prevails and counterinformation never sees the light of day. Informal interdepartmental interaction helps protect us from ourselves and inadvertent groupthink while also providing an opportunity to dig up the unknown unknowns. Interdepartmental interaction can serve as the "outside forces" within a company by informally creating oversight so that radars are given a better chance of early detection and there is an increased likelihood of an employee stepping up to say, "Something just doesn't feel right," even if that employee may be within the lowest of ranks.

5. Diversity Awareness

Getting to know an "other" is not easy and takes mental, rational energy. More and more companies are establishing mandatory diversity training classes without clearly establishing a motivation. Employees often attend the training to check a box or because they are providing the favor of inclusion to an underrepresented group. When we think of training as for the benefit of underrepresented groups, we tend to make it trite and likely to succumb to gravitational forces.

Just like the lunches, and likely even more so due to sharing of unique perspectives, the real benefit may be to those who don't belong to underrepresented groups; these training classes are free opportunities to expand their radars and allow them to purposefully grow. New perspectives are out there for their taking, and all that is required is awareness and mental energy to accept the new seeds.

Opportunities for diversity training are present in many hidden places as well by joining groups that are foreign to us, seeking stories of those that are different from us, listening to understand the perspective of those from an opposing party, and asking others about interests that may be alien to our own: *What's it like to be (blank)? What's it like to have (blank)? Tell me why you did that. Tell me why you think that.* Listening is not meant to differentiate right from wrong but rather to plant seeds that may later germinate in our future selves.

6. Sharing Our Stories (For Everyone— Not Just the High Profile)

Stories are important and often hidden. At times, we may feel ashamed to tell our stories, thinking they don't measure up to the flavor of the month. Measuring up, like doing the right thing, however, is dependent on which pond we are swimming in. It's easy to get lost in our little worlds. At one of my first jobs after law school, I worked in a law firm where I was a small fish. Day in and day out I was surrounded by a perfectionist culture where at times discussion centered around who had the most ceiling tiles in their office (a measure of success). It was my pond at the time, and I didn't know what I didn't know. Things like ceiling tiles became stressors.

What dug up an unknown unknown for me, however, was an inadvertent bus ride home. I was stuck at work without a car, and my only option was to take the "old-school city bus" home. It was a unique slice of life for me to see. That bus was packed with flavor. I recall one man, clearly drunk, stumbling to light a cigarette. He stumbled up and down the aisle, trying to light the cigarette, often falling to the side just as the flame was about to hit the firestick. I could feel the thoughts of the other passengers: *Please, please don't let that thing light.*

Finally, it did light, and a collective groan was let out by the passengers. The man was likely oblivious to what he was doing but was at least kind enough to proceed to the back and open a window. I was worried about ceiling tiles while others were just worried about surviving.

Unknown unknowns were dug up that day: *Wow, I actually have it pretty good* and *maybe this job just isn't for me.*

We all have stories to tell, and those stories are important opportunities for us to gain new perspective, since we often get lost in the isolation of our little worlds that largely exist in our own heads.

My company provides storytelling sessions led by senior employees as a way for other employees to get to know them. It's a way to put seeds into the environment for radar expansion. Stories of senior employees are great and helpful, but I'm particularly interested to hear the stories of the rank and file: those who may have had to overcome a few more obstacles in life; those whose seeds are worn, discolored, and cracked; those whose seeds have the potential to germinate into a one-of-a-kind flower on our radars. All of our stories are important to others, but it's often the stories of those we value the least that provide the most perspective.

My children's elementary school had a person-of-the-week presentation every Friday, during which one of the kids shared his or her story. Maybe we need to bring a little elementary school magic into the workplace.

7. Sharing and Working toward a Common Goal

As Sapolsky has discussed, one of the ways social psychologists break down the us-versus-them mentality is to come together in pursuit of a common goal. It's a two-part interaction: 1) merging different groups with different perspectives, and 2) doing so in pursuit of a common goal. The pursuit of a common goal provides an unstructured opportunity for awareness that we share commonality with someone not so common. The working together toward a goal enables invisible barriers to unconsciously erode in an automatic and emotional manner, unlike structured perspective taking, which requires more mental energy from the rational brain. When we work together with others toward a mutual objective, we break down barriers through osmosis.

This happened with my daughter during the Outward Bound wilderness program, described more fully later in this book. My daughter was heading down the wrong path in middle school, and my wife and I decided she needed to spend the summer in a different environment. We signed her up for a monthlong leadership program in the Boundary Waters Canoe Area. She went into the program kicking and screaming, predicting that she was going to get stuck spending a month in the wilderness with girls who think it's cool to be bisexual. "They are all f———ing different than me," she screamed before the adventure. "Those girls are just not like me. Please, please don't make me go with them," she said. "I'm not like them."

She reluctantly went on the adventure, and after the program ended, I asked her whom she had clicked with most. She said, "Stephanie and Ingrid." She then paused and said, "And you know, they are bisexual."

"Huh," I said. "Do you remember what you said to me about bisexual girls a few months ago?"

She thought about it and said, "Hmmm."

8. Minimizing Group Differences

Another way to break down invisible barriers is to minimize group differences by consciously creating diversity within teams. We can do this by structuring our departments so we at times work with those with whom we may not otherwise interact. We thereby can create unique opportunities to experience that we are all not so different; that we each have mothers and fathers who may not be so perfect; that we may have siblings who struggle with illness; that we all need to at times push ourselves just to get through the day; that we all have fabulous moments of insight, achievement, or connecting with others; that we all experience not-so-fabulous moments of selfishness, failure and just being a jerk; that we are all at times lonely and unfulfilled; and that we "eat, sleep, and shit" just like everyone else.

Seeing an "other" as an individual can be a transformational experience of empathy. From Mother Theresa ("If I look at the mass I will never act; if I look at the one, I will") to Joseph Stalin ("Death of one man is a tragedy; death of millions is a statistic"), there is vast understanding that getting to know an "other" outside of the group can change our worlds of perspective.

9. Removing Hierarchical Barriers

Just as it's important to build diversity into teams, it's also important to consciously break down company caste systems. Accountability is important for growth and development, but it needs to go both ways. Companies are separate entities, just like individuals on the path toward growth and creation. Companies evolve as purposefully as the individuals within it purposefully evolve. Each person shares the power of their decision—no one is more or less important for the growth of the whole. When caste systems are empowered, the lower-tiered caste members tend to defer their purpose and give away their power to those up the chain. But power can only be derived when others give it away. This doesn't mean there should not be a chain of command but that each employee, no matter the rank, should remain aware of where his or her purpose lies or it will likely default up the chain.

Our individual purpose, and hence our creation, is always our decision. It is our primary source of power. There is no caste system in purpose. Everyone wields the same power. Joe Darby, the lowest-ranking member in his unit, transformed the lives of many by holding on to his power and deciding his purpose would not go toward something he "just knew was wrong."

Loosening the labels and command structure differential within a company may make it easier for the rank and file to recognize that they each wield unique powers of perspective and that power is too important to blindly give away. Company interaction between the highs and the lows of the caste system go a long way toward breaking down those barriers, as do CEOs who willingly share their messes, failures, insecurities, and commonalities.

10. Listen to Those Below

In a similar manner, it is vital for those up the chain to listen to those in the trenches. The unknown unknowns are usually dug up by those in the field. If they are dug up with no place to go, they are useless.

Companies often create mechanisms for feedback, but those mechanisms often become trite. One hotline is not enough. As described earlier in Part 1 of this book, a company whose mission was to "strive to be recognized by our stake holders as setting the standard among the world's great companies for integrity and principled performance" set up a company hotline to ensure that unprincipled behavior would not go unnoticed. That hotline received thousands of complaints of unprincipled behavior, particularly in one department. Unfortunately, however, the company culture of profits got in the way, and the complaints fell on deaf ears. The hotline was ringing, but there was no one to answer, and the unprincipled behavior continued for years.

In hindsight, multiple hotlines may have been helpful, as sometimes radars can be down for maintenance.

11. Rotate Those in Charge of Monitoring the DTRT Radars

All of our radars can at times be down for maintenance, often because our defaults become too pervasive. Company awareness entails acknowledging that we are all works in progress, that our radars are not always working at full capacity or even working at all. Rotating those who monitor the company radar entails acknowledging the importance of DTRT and building in safeguards for its oversight.

Many companies use this approach by rotating those who work with particular vendors to avoid the temptation to become too cozy, thereby hurting competition and profits. Companies also use this approach by rotating COO responsibility to ensure fresh eyes on the companies' processes. It is critical to ensure the DTRT team is rotated to maximize efforts to flesh out the unknown unknowns and ensure that employees are empowered to speak their truth.

12. Encourage Vulnerability

Have you ever been on a conference call or in a meeting when something just didn't make sense or you didn't understand what was being said? How often did you speak out? It is likely that this situation has occurred to all of us and also likely that only 10 percent of us stepped up to say something. I've been doing legal work for twenty-five years, as mentioned previously, and at times, it still causes me pause to speak out.

Fear of failure, fear of looking stupid, fear of being the center of attention—fear, fear, fear. It's much easier to sit back and go with the default of doing nothing. That's human nature, as we are told by social psychologists.

But we can make it easier. And we know how to do that: ten percent turns into 90 percent when someone else leads the way. We can build into our companies the victim calling out and the coteacher modeling, but this will not happen without awareness.

We can create a daily ILST (I Looked Stupid Today) award for those employees who took a chance and spoke out at the risk of looking stupid.

We can create a monthly FTSOC (First to Speak Out Club) that provides benefits such as extra paid-time-off days or gift cards or opportunities to share a message to those who were first to speak up about an issue.

We can create an ETMC (Embrace the Mess Club) that provides opportunities for employees to share their messes and resulting growth impact.

We can create company incentives that encourage modeling against the default in novel and creative ways.

But it will not happen without awareness.

13. Micromanaging—My Radar Sees Everything

Micromanaging is a naive belief that our radar is all-powerful and sees everything. It is a lose-lose proposition for uncovering the unknown unknowns. Not only does it lock in place the radar of the manager, it shuts down the radar of the managed. There is no opportunity for the managed to spread his seeds or the manager to till her soil for new growth.

My first job as an attorney was for a micromanager. Because of this, I questioned everything I did, often freezing with inaction.

How is he going to receive my writing? I better rewrite this, I thought over and over. Rather than doing, failing, and learning, I was frozen in the pursuit of illusory perfection. The irony of the situation, in hindsight, is that he didn't even know what he wanted. I was trying to seek perfection in a moving target.

And that is how it is with life generally. The target is always moving. There is no other way. Change is the name of the game. Rather than seeking perfection in ourselves as moving targets or, worse yet, trying to pass off our perfection to others, we may be better off acknowledging that there is no target in life—just movement.

And the best way to capture movement is through multiple radars. When we micromanage, we shut down the auxiliary radars.

14. Reminders

If there is one key takeaway from the social psychologists, it's that 90 percent of us travel through life with blinders on—sleepwalking. We decide and create through the default of others. Taking the blinders off and waking up is extremely difficult. No one will ever fully wake up, but no one ever said that is the goal. The goal is awareness—awareness that we live with blinders on and most of the time walk around half asleep. When we sleepwalk, we let go of the reins and the horses run wild. Awareness lets us take back the reins to drive with purpose.

Reminders are there to say, "Wake up and grab the reins."

For reminders to work effectively, however, they must be in open places and rearranged over time. If we splash reminders all over the company and don't move them around, they will become trite and unnoticed, like the half-completed construction project in your house that after time goes unnoticed. For reminders to work, they should be moved around in novel and creative ways.

CHAPTER 21

Tools for Expanding Employees' Radars

WE KNOW FROM the social psychologists that expanding our radars is difficult, very difficult. A very small percentage of us—we know by now the number—step up on our own volition when gravity keeps the matter below our radars, whether it be helping a stranger in the street, going against the direction of a researcher, or spending the mental energy to sympathize with an "other."

From the research and through common sense and experience, we know there are ways we can proactively expand our radars, building upon our being to grow and evolve in a purposeful manner.

But without one central ingredient, purposeful evolution and growth are impossible. Without awareness that we are decision-making machines and our decisions are derived from our purpose—our personal mission statement—we will evolve at the whims of others. Without awareness, our radars will evolve at the rate of the defaults of those to whom we are attached. Our radars go into "sleep" mode, changing at the whims of other "software engineers."

With awareness, we become our own software engineers.

We write our own programs: how sensitive our instruments will be, to what extent they will be tuned, who has permission to coprogram. Awareness is an acknowledgment that we don't have the answers, just the ability to ask the questions and evolve through the process.

The following are twelve tools we can use to increase our personal awareness and become our own radar software engineers.

1. Reminders

Purposeful self-creation is hard—extremely hard. The power structures of society are built upon mechanisms to steal our power. The messages are constant:

- We have the answer to your malcontent.
- We have the answer for your fear.
- We have a plan for your wealth.
- We have the system to make you smarter.
- We have the schedule to make you more skilled.

The comparisons are constant as well:

- My neighbors' kid made the "A" team, is first chair in band, is a straight-A student, got into an Ivy League college, is engaged…
- He has a fancier job title; her office is bigger; she drives a nicer car; she is liked more than me…
- He has more "followers" than me, she got more "up-votes"…

It never ends—the comparisons, the betterment, the feeling of lack as compared to others. It is challenging not to give in to it. It is constant. It is society's culture.

But just as we created rocket ships to escape gravity, we have ways to help us fight society's default gravity. And just like the rocket ship, constant propulsion is required.

We need daily reminders to help with our constant propulsion, for example:

- Hindus wear a dot between their eyes as a constant reminder to use and cultivate spiritual vision.
- Muslims pray five times a day at set times as reminders of connection to each other.
- Christians attend church regularly to stay attuned and prevent backsliding.
- Fitness enthusiasts establish set routines to ensure continuity of health.
- Companies post visual reminders to do the right thing to keep integrity on par with profits.
- Individuals pray every night to keep perspective and establish gratitude.
- Many eat with mindfulness to remember we are materially interconnected.
- Some meditate in the shower to feel and appreciate our sensuality.
- Many listen intently to nature as reminders that we are not alone.
- Others contemplate each *individual* tree, plant, and rock as representations of the beauty of our uniqueness.

There is no shortage of rituals to keep the consistency, because, just as in the case of the rocket ship, one minute of letting up sends us back down. Gravity wins until we escape it.

In addition to rituals, having other people and systems to hold us accountable may prove effective in fighting gravity. It's too easy to succumb to the constant pressure; it's almost impossible not to. We will succumb. When we do, we need others to say, "Hey, wake up. What are you doing, man? You're succumbing to the default."

Well, they probably won't say that. It will be more like, "Who cares if your kid didn't make the 'A' team? Do you really care if your office has fewer ceiling tiles than your next-door neighbor's? Do we really need to pay for the Huggies when the Luvs are half the price?"

We are there to hold each other accountable because we will all succumb.

2. The Company You Keep

Rituals and accountability help us fight the gravity of our defaults. We know why rituals and accountability are so helpful: They cause the ninety-ten inversion. They are the victim calling out for help, the coteacher stopping the trial. They are the radar helpers, those around us helping our radars activate when we are in sleep mode.

They are the company we keep. Buddha and the social psychologists agree: "If it is purposeful change you seek, there is no ingredient more important than the company you keep."

Choose your friends wisely. If they don't share your vision for who you want to be, find new ones. Choose your job wisely. You likely spend more than half of your waking hours at your job. If your company does not share your vision for who you want to be, find a new one.

There is ultimately only one person who cares about the creation of you. If you let go of the reins, you will have wandering horses directing your path. Make it easier on yourself to cause your radar to blink when the time arrives. It's much easier to occasionally cull the company you keep than monitor your radar every minute of every day.

Consider wise selection of your company as giving your radar some needed downtime.

3. Humility

The death knell to increasing our awareness is arrogance, thinking we already have the answers. When we think we know all there is to know, our radars become maxed out; there is no room for growth. Our radars are not catered to, they are not watered, they are shut down to newcomers. Often the more we achieve, the more we accumulate (whether knowledge or things); or the larger our influence, the more apt we are to lose our humility. Situations tell us how great we are. Our things tell us the extent to which we surpass others. Our knowledge makes us superior. Our generosity makes us a finer class of person. Or so we think. We think we are already "there." But where are we? We lose sight of the process and become enthralled with the destination. The destination becomes the answer. We miss life occurring while we sit fascinated by the prize.

Humility is our statement that we are living in the journey, ripe for change, and eager for growth. Humility is what allows us to take an interest in someone else, listen to their stories, and allow them to plant their seeds within us. Humility is the radar saying we've only just begun—and there is nowhere to go. We are works in progress.

4. Questions before Answers

Our questioning creates the process of life. Questions are what plant the seeds of growth. They are what allow us to start the journey. The questions start us out. The answers finish us up. And the process continues.

Answers presuppose a destination. There can be no right or wrong without a destination.

- If living long is the destination, eating healthy may be right. If feeling good in the moment is the destination, eating healthy may be wrong.
- If loosening up is the destination, having a few drinks may be right. If keeping control is the destination, having a few drinks may be wrong.
- If accumulating is the destination, ruthlessness may be right. If connection with others is the destination, ruthlessness may be wrong.
- If survival is the destination, destruction may be right. If growth is the destination, destruction may be wrong.

Questions provide the journey: Why are you eating that? Why are you pounding down the drinks? Why are you so intensely focused? Why did you start that war?

Answers are for doing; questions are for being. Questions are the seeds we plant to help our radars grow. Answers provide us with a destination. Without questions, there would be no journey, nothing to seek.

My son is constantly asking questions: "Why are you wearing those shoes? How long does it take to bike to work? Why do you bike to work? Why do cars need gas? Why can't I jump high enough to slam-dunk a basketball?" The questions are endless. And it is exhausting. He is growing. He is expanding. It is happening right before our eyes, and it would be easy to miss if it weren't for the questions.

No matter how exhausting, annoying, or time-consuming we think they may be, questions from others are them simply saying, "Hey, I'm growing, looking to expand my radar." How can we not respect that?

The same applies to us: holding back our questions means leaving our tools in the box. If you value growth, ask your questions and keep asking; bring out the tools. Often the only dumb question is the one not asked. It may have been one that changed the world or, more importantly, changed you.

5. Vulnerability

I wasn't like most other boys growing up: I didn't want to be a professional athlete. What I wanted to be was a dad. I recall walking through the health club and looking at the dads who had their kids with them—specifically, the ones who had the kids hold their hands as they walked through the club. I recall thinking to myself, *Yep, that's what I want to be when I get older. I want to be a dad. No question.*

I have been lucky enough to become a dad three times over. It was what both my wife, Kathleen, and I wanted more than anything—to be parents, and to be good parents, the absolute best we could be. For seventeen years, this is where we have spent most of our time and energy—doing our best for our kids and family. Work and family: that has been our mantra. And that is about all we have done.

We had dreams of being a happy family, with the kids involved in activities and us cheering them on. Dreams of friends, sleepovers, and fun. Dreams of their proceeding through school and advancing to college, eventually moving out and living on their own. After we got the news about our son, that his life would likely take a different, nontraditional path, it took a while, but we regrouped. Our focus was to help him close the developmental gap; we "threw the kitchen sink at it." And from there, for the next six or seven years, things proceeded more or less according to plan. School, activities, and work. We were a family going to events together as a unit of five and loving every minute of it. We were involved in all the school activities, attended all the swim meets. We did everything as a family. It was everything we had dreamed—so, so wonderful. I recall often thinking, *How do families deal with kids moving out of the house? It is just so incredible to be together as a family.*

It made me sad just to think about the kids growing up and moving on. I didn't want it to end. Until it stopped. Our oldest daughter became more anxious and depressed, stopped going to school, and eventually ended up in and out of hospitals and residential facilities, as I have discussed. We spent years almost exclusively focusing on trying to help her close her mental health gap. But we had little success. No therapy was working; no medication was working. She had spurts of progress but invariably would end up back in the hospital. And as we were spending our energy on her mental health, our middle daughter started to rebel. There were calls from school every week: "Your daughter is cheating on tests, your daughter is a leader (but in the wrong way), your daughter is disrespectful to staff."

Soon she dropped out of her activities and just wanted to hang out with her friends, vaping and smoking pot. She disrespected anyone in authority. She was headed down the wrong path, fast.

We had no energy or ability to focus on her. But she was demanding it. She was the forgotten piece in our family. We lost sight of her, and she was having none of it. Kathleen and I regrouped and turned our energy toward her. We decided we needed to send her away for the summer. I looked into various options. I remembered as a kid hearing about a program called Outward Bound. I searched for it on the internet, and sure enough they had a program for teenagers just like her, kids beginning to head down the wrong path who needed a little encouragement to turn the ship around. It was called the Intercept Program.

I did some more investigating. I called the Outward Bound

program staff and discussed the program's fit for our daughter. I learned about a thirty-day survival course in the Boundary Waters Canoe Area, where a group of seven teenage girls and two counselors live in the wilderness.

"The hardest thing she will ever do, and probably the most impactful thing she will ever do," the staff member said.

Sounded fantastic—I loved it, and I loved it for her. There was only one problem. She did not want to go.

"No way you are taking my summer from me," she said. "No f——ing way. You are not taking me away from my friends. I'm not f——ing going. I hate you guys…you are the absolute worst parents. Look at what you have done to all of us…look how screwed up our family is, and it is because of you."

Wow. That hit home. Our family was screwed up. My dream of becoming a great dad or even a good dad was now a faded memory. The days of never wanting parenthood and the family to run their course were now gone. Life had turned on a dime. Day after day, Kathleen and I either asked or thought, *What have we done to screw this up so badly—one kid with cognitive and behavioral issues, another with mental health issues, and another who is flat-out rebelling?*

The parent-of-the-year award had our names written all over it—for last place. We knew we needed to do something for our middle daughter. Get her into a different scene. So I put down the deposit, and we trusted that when the time came, she would go. The days and weeks passed, and she would not even acknowledge that Boundary Waters was a possibility. She didn't tell her friends. She kept acting as if her summer would be spent at home with her friends, just hanging out.

Prior to being officially accepted into the program, a telephone interview with the Outward Bound staff was required to make sure the students could handle the adventure.

How is this going to work? my wife and I thought.

The time for the interview finally arrived. We were both sitting on needles to see what would happen. We handed her the telephone, and she did it: She participated in the interview. She was honest. She engaged.

Huh, a good sign, we thought. *Deep down she must know this is right for her.*

Or was that just our wishful thinking? The school year then started winding down. We needed to start preparing her for the trip. There was a two-page list of gear that needed to be purchased for her monthlong adventure in the rugged terrain. She still refused to engage.

"I don't care. I don't need any of that shit."

So Kathleen went shopping for the gear by herself. S (I will identify our daughter by her first initial to protect her privacy) would not try on any clothes; she would not even look at the equipment. We had bought it all trusting she would go.

Finally, the night before we needed to drive her to Duluth to meet the rest of the kids, who were flying from all over the country, and the staff for the orientation and subsequent trip north to the Boundary Waters, I picked her up from a night out with her friends. She was crying her eyes out and hugging her friends. I knew then that she was going. Deep down she knew she needed to go. We were on our way.

The day finally arrived. We packed up the van, and she reluctantly climbed in. The entire drive was either filled with tears or threats of never talking to us again: "You are ruining my life. I hate you. I hate you so much. You have screwed up all of our lives. Worst parents ever."

Finally, we arrived at the Duluth airport. We knew we had found our crew, because it looked as if we had just walked into Woodstock: long beards, tie-dye shirts, hiking boots. And then in walks in our daughter, looking as though she were going to a beauty pageant: eye shadow, eyeliner (lots of it), rouge, lipstick, and, of course, designer clothes. She walked in, stood in the corner with her arms crossed, and just eyed everyone else.

"Oh my f——ing…"

Crying and more crying. Finally, one of the counselors pulled her aside for a quick pep talk. She rolled her eyes and proceeded back to her corner. She sat there for a minute. Then one of the other girls walked up to her and said, "You know they don't allow makeup out there."

The girl walked away, and our daughter responded with the finger.

Soon they gathered together for introductions. We watched. Because we were the only family from Minnesota (all of the other kids said goodbye to their parents at the airport before they flew in from other states), we were able to hang around until the kids boarded vans to proceed up north. During the introductions, our daughter continued to stand back with arms crossed, still refusing to put on the camp gear. One of the leaders then started asking questions of the teenagers after they gathered into a group.

"What is something that you will not be permitted to have in the wilderness?" he asked.

"Cell phones," one kid replied.

"Yep," the counselor responded. "What else?"

Then a boy said loudly, "Marijuana."

The kids started to laugh, and we looked at our daughter. She was grinning ear to ear. We could see her thinking, *OK, these might be my people.*

She then started to change out of her designer clothes and into her camp gear. The program was a monthlong adventure where we (the parents) would hear nothing except for a check-in at the halfway point, an hourlong phone call with the counselors to get an overview of how the first half of the expedition was proceeding.

During that entire two weeks, Kathleen was a wreck. She checked the weather map every day and asked me at least three times a day, "I wonder how she is? Tim, how do you think she is doing?"

"How am I supposed to know?" I responded.

The check-in day was now just around the corner. It was the Sunday after the Fourth of July. On that Friday, however, we received an email from the Outward Bound staff: "Don't be alarmed..." it started out.

You never want to open an email that begins with those words, especially when your kid is in the Boundary Waters alone for a month and you have not heard from her for two weeks. The email continued: "One of the kids in one of the groups has walked out of the campsite and is missing. We don't want you to be alarmed. You may hear about it on the news or internet. It does not involve your daughter or her group."

Wow, oh my God. What have we done? Did we send her to some camp that is so horrible that kids run away? They can't make a last-place parent-of-the-year last enough for us. We try and try so hard, and we just seem to be messing this parenting thing up so badly.

Finally, the Sunday of our phone call check-in with the counselors came around.

"She's doing OK," they said. "Don't think she is loving it. But she is really embracing the physical parts of the challenges. It was one hundred degrees outside during the rock climbing adventure, and she begged us to go up again. Everyone else just sat under the shade. She's loving the physical challenge."

OK, we thought. *She is doing OK. Maybe we can move up from last place parent-of-the-year club.*

It was two more weeks before the program ended. Homework was required of us. We needed to prepare for our own weekend adventure. Prior to the trip ending, the parents were instructed to arrive on Thursday to undergo a "mini–Outward Bound experience." It would be similar to what the girls were doing in the wilderness, only we would do it in a conference center over a period of three days.

We arrived for the parent minicourse. The kids were back from the trip and in town to do a service project. The counselors, who had been with the girls during the trip, were now at the conference center with the parents. We introduced ourselves to one of the counselors as we walked in.

"We are S's parents. How'd she do?" I immediately asked, thinking the worst was to come.

"I think it was OK. I wouldn't say she loved it, but I think she appreciated it."

I said, "Do you think she would ever do it again?"

Long pause, and then she said, "No."

We then had breakfast and got to know some of the other parents. After breakfast, we assembled with the other parents of the kids in her group and the counselors to start the minicourse. We gathered around a circle, talking about our kids, why they were there and what we were hoping to get out of it. The counselors then started talking about their monthlong adventure with the kids. The parents were fishing for information.

"You'll get to see them in three days, I promise," was the often-cited response during that early period. "This is your experience. You'll meet with your daughters soon, I promise."

One of the counselors explained, "This entire journey for the girls has been about growth and perception change, helping them become independent and realizing that they are responsible for their environment. At first, we show them how to camp, and then slowly they come to be on their own: navigating, gathering firewood, cooking, building the tent, canoeing. If they want to paddle slowly, then we go slowly but don't get to the destination until late at night. Soon they realize that if they don't get to camp until late at night, setting up the tents, making fire, and cooking will be pretty tough in the pitch-black night. They soon learn to paddle faster. Every night after dinner we have group time—we share, learn, and connect. Where are they in life? Where do they want to be, and how can they get there? They hold each other accountable. They help each other gain perspective. They soon realize they are their own keepers, while at the same time they are there for each other."

Another counselor then said, "Here is your first exercise; it was the girls' first exercise, and it is your first exercise. Take out a piece of paper, and write down what your relationship was like with your daughter five years ago and what it is like now. What has changed?"

We each took time to think and write. Then we proceeded to share. My time came to share and I—wow, something happened. I broke down. I mean really broke down. I got two words out and started crying. Two more and then more crying. I thought they would move on, but they just waited.

"Take as long as you need," they said.

Two more words and more breaking down.

What the heck? I thought. *Get it together.*

But I couldn't control it. After about five minutes of sitting there under the spotlight like a wreck, I think I got it out: "Five years ago we were a happy family. Now her sister is in a mental hospital, and her brother is just struggling to get by, and everything is so hard for him. S is stuck in the middle. She didn't do anything wrong. She didn't do anything wrong. None of us did anything wrong. What has happened? It all fell apart."

Whew, I thought. *What happened there? All right, let's get it together and move on.*

We took a break. The next part of this exercise entailed the parents saying what they appreciated about each other.

All right, we're past my breakdown, I thought.

Not so fast. One after another the other parents responded: "I appreciate what you just did, Tim."

Another: "I feel like it gave me permission to feel."

Another: "It opened me up. Thank you for doing that."

For doing what? I thought. *I couldn't help it.*

Later one of the other parents came up to me and said, "I

called my wife to tell her about how inspired I was by what you did. It really affected me. I just wish I could open up like that."

I said, "I didn't do anything—really, really, I didn't."

"Yes, you did," he said.

After another hour, one of the counselors came up to me. "Tim, I just happened to overhear your group. I had a similar experience to yours growing up. What you did opened up something in me."

"What? I didn't do anything."

I had never experienced anything like this before. I now realize what I did. I broke open, and that gave others permission to break open. Pain that had been trapped was now starting to emerge. All of our seeds cracked that day. Mine just happened to be the first.

There was so much energy and love in that conference center that weekend. You could feel it. Energy was oozing out of so many broken seeds.

This is what the adventure was about: opening up, connecting, sharing, and growing.

The next day started with a slideshow of some of the groups and a description of the program and how it came to be. It was started by a gentleman in Germany after WWII who was looking to change the trajectory of German society and start a path toward rebirth. He was a survivor of the war looking to rebuild, and he was also blind.

His plan: create a culture where we come together with common purpose for mutual growth.

His mission statement: "Your disability is your opportunity."

That weekend was transformational. I walked in thinking, *Poor me. Why is all this happening?*

I left smiling. *Wow, we are blessed with an unbelievable, remarkable opportunity for growth. And we are starting to see the growth and experience parts of ourselves never before imaginable—connectivity, courage, and the indescribable feeling generated by sharing our "good stuff."*

I often think back to the day of breakdown. It was a day of vulnerability. It was a day I never would have desired, certainly never could have planned. But everything changed because of it. My seed cracked wide open. I have learned to appreciate the power of vulnerability, the cracking of our seeds. It is the way we share ourselves with others. We all want the good stuff from each other. Not the outer shell. The good stuff from inside. Yet many of us walk around with shells intact. And when they inevitably crack, we immediately work to repair them. We live as if our goal is to finish life with seeds fully intact.

But what good are fully intact seeds? They can't share or grow. They sit isolated and eventually wither away with the good stuff locked inside. But cracked seeds—they let the good stuff flow. They repopulate. They grow and grow and grow and grow.

We saw our daughter that Sunday. The buildup of not seeing her for a month, then waiting three days while hearing about the adventure and the stories from the parents of the other kids was starting to become unbearable. We all kept asking, "When are they arriving?"

"Just wait," they said. "Your program is not done."

"Please can you just tell us a little more about their experience? Show us a few pictures, at least?" we would ask.

"Trust us," they would say. "You'll get much more out of it this way."

"But we can't wait any longer!" one of the moms would cry out. "We need to see our babies."

Finally, they arrived in vans. The kids had all apparently vowed not to talk to the parents who sent them away. They had planned to play it tough. But the doors opened, and the cracked-seed campers flew out of the van to their awaiting cracked-seed parents.

Playing it tough never stood a chance.

And as for the adventure, after it all soaked in, S has said on a number of occasions, "No question about it. That was the best month of my life."

6. Messes

Messes are signs that our defaults may be in conflict with our reality. They are signs that our life purpose may have met a roadblock. For example:

- If our life purpose is to live long, sickness and disease are going to create a mess of us.
- If our life purpose is to prosper, not doing better than our neighbor is going to create a mess of us.
- If our life purpose is to be kind, others walking all over us is going to create a mess of us.
- If our life purpose is to be generous, others taking advantage of us is going to create a mess of us.
- If our life purpose is anything that requires a result, our life at some point is going to be a mess.

We all have messes in our lives. As long as there are defaults, there will be messes. Messes are life communicating with us. They are life asking us to reexamine our defaults. If we continually get messed up when someone outperforms us, life may be asking us/begging us to reexamine our life purpose of prosperity. After we challenge that default and find purpose in something else, we may slowly start to see that others outperforming us carries less and less of a sting and eventually fades away. It (others outperforming us) only has meaning because we gave purpose to its counterpart, prosperity (doing better than others). Take away its counterpart, and it becomes just another event.

Messes can be redescribed as opportunities. Opportunities

to examine our defaults and move on to new, more evolved defaults. The messier the mess, the more life may be communicating that it is time to reexamine our defaults. When the default is brought into awareness, it can be overcome. With persistence, it will eventually disappear. Dissolving one mess and moving on to another. That's how we grow.

We are all works in progress—beautiful messes.

7. Stop and Listen

When messes occur, it may be life calling us to stop and listen. Life reaching out to us individually. Messes are life echoing our thoughts back to us in the form of discomfort.

We often try to plow through them. When we get sick, we fight back. We try to beat it. But what if the sickness is simply asking us to stop and listen?

What am I to learn from this?

How can I use this sickness to experience more of myself?

It just may be when we stop and listen, we change our perspective and grow. We all get sick and eventually die, but we do not all learn and grow from the process. That is entirely up to us.

8. Change in Perspective

As Sapolsky has discussed, research shows that we often give ourselves the benefit of the doubt but rarely do so for others. Imagine that you are at a work function and you see twelve cans of Coke on a table. You grab one of them, thinking nothing of it. Later a colleague comes up to you as you are drinking the Coke and asks where you got it. You say, "I got it over there with the rest of the cans that were left out for grabs."

The colleague says, "Those weren't for grabs. I've got a group coming in for a presentation, and we need those Cokes."

Was your action of taking the Coke stealing? Likely not in your mind. You think, *Come on, we're at work. Things left out are up for grabs; that's just how it is. How was I to know?*

You give yourself the benefit of the doubt.

It wasn't stealing—I know me, and I wouldn't do that. It was an honest mistake.

What about if you were to witness this conversation as an observer of two colleagues? The colleague who took the Coke is someone you don't really like or trust—a rival of yours. You just see the tail end of the conversation: "I'm sorry, I didn't know those Cokes were for a meeting."

What's your first reaction in witnessing this interaction? Are you going to put in the work and rationalize your colleague's actions the same way you rationalize your actions? Or are you more prone to think, *Of course he would just take it without asking. That's just the kind of person he is?*

We often give ourselves and those in our group the benefit of the doubt through rationalization, because we know the backstory. We are willing to put in the mental energy to rationalize our actions, to keep the mental model of ourselves intact. But we rarely do so for others because it takes work. It takes mental energy to rationalize, and the closer we are to the situation, the less likely we are to do it.

In a series of experiments, summarized and described by Sapolsky, where people were asked if they would kill one person to save five if it meant pushing that one person on the train track to stop an oncoming train, 30 percent of respondents said they would do it. But if they could pull a lever to reroute the train to another track to kill the one to save the five, 60 percent of respondents said they would do it. And in another variation, 90 percent of respondents said they would be OK with inadvertently killing someone (accidentally bumping into the person and causing him to fall onto the track to stop the train) to save the five.

The outcomes are exactly the same: kill one person to save five. What differed was the intimacy and causality of the situation. The closer we are to the situation, the more emotional our responses tend to be. The more distant we are, the more logical we become. To put it another way, the closer we are to a situation, the more difficult it is to react rationally. For instance, in the Coke scenario, if we hear about the story from afar, we react rationally, giving the other the same benefit of the doubt we would give ourselves. If, however, we are personally involved, we are more likely to react emotionally and give ourselves the benefit of the doubt while labeling the other person.

When we are close to a situation, it takes mental energy to react rationally. We will often expend that mental energy if it means protecting the mental construct we have of ourselves.

But not so much for others—too much work. We rarely give *them* the same benefit of the doubt through rationalization.

It may be that we act that way because we think there is nothing in it for us. But there is always something in it for us. A change in perspective (seeing through another's eyes) and an expansion of our radars is something if we want it to be and are willing to put in the extra mental work.

9. Reserving Judgment

Not judging a situation is really an acknowledgment that we don't have the full story, an acknowledgment that there is another angle to the story. We know our backstories but almost never know the backstories of others.

Awareness is catching ourselves when we judge. There is always another side to the story. Can we walk into the middle of a movie and make an informed decision about it? When we walk into the middle of a movie, we acknowledge we don't know its backstory, so we often leave and reserve judgment.

In a similar manner, when we watch a movie, we tend to empathize with the hero because we have been shown his story. But what about the villain? We are almost never shown the villain's history. Why? Because then we would empathize with him as well.

Awareness is recognizing that everyone has a history. How often do we leave a juicy life situation and reserve judgment, thinking, *I don't know the full backstory, so I'll just step out of these "movie doors"?*

We never know the full history of another, and yet we are often eager to judge. How does seeing only the middle of the movie help us make purposeful decisions? When we decide from the middle of the movie, we prevent ourselves from seeing the scene from a different angle, an angle with a backstory, an angle that just could be food for our radar's growth.

10. Curiosity

Curiosity killed the cat. That's one way of looking at it. The day will come when we all die. It's part of the process. Something we have to do. Die and decide—the only two things we have to do in life.

We can try to tame our curiosity and postpone our killing. But once we open the door to our birdcages and fly out to see the world, it's hard to keep us in there. There is something within us that eventually seeks to explore new frontiers—new frontiers that can kill us.

I remember walking out of the movie *Everest*, the story of mountain climbers who got caught in a storm and died while on the mountain. The movie went to great lengths to explain the risks of the climb: freezing temperatures, falling rocks, loose footing, avalanches, huge crevices, lack of oxygen, bottlenecks, unexpected storms, lack of food, lack of water. Yet, despite the significant risk of death in doing something with no tangible reward, there are waiting lists of climbers.

It makes no sense. Why would anyone do that? For what? As I walked out of the movie theater, I overheard a couple conversing and expressing that sentiment: "I don't understand why anyone would do that. For what? Why risk your life to climb a mountain? I hate to say it, but they got what they deserved."

That is one way of looking at it. But there is obviously another way, or there would not be a waiting list of climbers willing to risk death for no tangible reward. I can only surmise that for the climbers the mountain is symbolic of leaving the birdcage. They risk their lives for the adventure, the process that causes them to experience aspects of themselves that only exist as potential. They risk their lives for growth.

It seems illogical, but maybe not that illogical. We all die; it's just a matter of time. We all grow; it's just a matter of the rate. Maybe they are just risking the time for the rate.

Curiosity could just be life's inherent motivator for growth. Our inherent desire to expand our radars. We can tame it to postpone our killing. We can aggressively use it to speed up our growth. Or, with awareness, we can do a little of both.

11. Give and Receive

There are only two things we have to do in life—die and decide. When we decide, we create. We have to do it. And we have to do it uniquely. It's really the only thing we know for sure in life. We have to create in our own unique way.

That is our mandatory gift to each other. We put our unique creations out there just by living.

The infinite number of gifts out there are waiting to be received, a smorgasbord of presents. Gifts are automatic. Reception is not. Our choice comes in which gifts we *receive*. Awareness is our ability to receive purposefully.

12. Wisdom

For me, one of the sure signs that someone is wise is that they readily acknowledge that they don't know. We've come a long way in knowing things. But it seems the more we know, the more we realize the breadth of the unknown.

- We previously knew that the Earth was the center of the universe, until we didn't.
- We previously knew that the atom was the smallest element, until we continued to discover yet smaller and smaller elements.
- We previously knew that light consisted of a wave, until someone else knew it consisted of a particle, until someone else knew the particle was a portion of the wave existing as potential.
- We previously knew reality was a separate "existence," until we knew reality is dependent on the observer.
- We previously knew that cow's milk was a necessary part of the food groups, until we knew it may be harmful to some people.
- We previously knew that being a strict parent was the correct way to parent, until we knew it could lead to rebellion.
- We then knew empowerment was the key to parenting, until we knew it could lead to entitlement.

It seems the more we know, the more we realize how much we don't know. The more we learn about the fundamental nature of existence, particularly from the field of quantum physics, the more we uncover our connectedness. Nothing exists in a state by itself. The observer impacts the observed.

Our radars expand when we acknowledge the vast universe of unknowns. We open ourselves to new knowledge. We're open to redoing. We're open to being wrong. We're open to exploring. We're open to sharing. We're open to totally new ways of thinking—like when we discovered that light is not just a particle or a wave but both parts of each other, one simply existing as potential until acted upon.

Sometimes the wisest are the first to acknowledge they are the dumbest, in that they know almost nothing. And when we recognize we know almost nothing, we open up ourselves to learn things in new ways.

Conclusion

There are only two things that any of us know for sure: we must die, and we must decide. Deciding leads to creation. We have no control over whether we create. It is something we must do simply by being alive. We do, however, have control over *how* we create. This is done through purposeful decision-making.

It is the most important thing any of us will do. It is also the thing most of us are likely to outsource to another. We outsource for many reasons, fear included, but mostly we outsource because we are asleep. We make decisions based on defaults that we have accumulated through the years, often like half-completed home projects that over time simply blend in and fall out of awareness. We are marching to the beat of someone else's drum and are not even aware of it.

Most of the time we don't see the effects of our group sleepwalking. But its effects rear their heads when novel situations require unique action. In those novel situations, most of us simply go with the flow and either don't see the situation for what it is or are too fearful to act. It's not hard to understand why three officers stood by and did nothing when George Floyd was being mercilessly detained. That situation required unique action.

Our sleepwalking also appears when we experience messes in our lives. Messes are life's alarm clock intended to wake us from our slumber. When we ignore the messes, we press life's snooze button.

I'm tired, not quite ready to wake up.

We can indefinitely press life snooze if we so choose. We can even try to turn the alarm off all together. But as long as we are alive, there will always be decisions and their subsequent creations—and alarms signaling the possibility of a new way.

With awareness, constant reminders, and an attention to the company we keep, we may have the courage to avoid hitting snooze or attempting to turn off the alarm. Awareness is not easy, but with it, magic awaits to transform our unique potential into reality.

And finally, awareness allows us collectively to be open to new ideas, perspectives, and thoughts that lead to the creation of a company culture through which the unknown unknowns begin to blink on our individual and collective (i.e., company's) radar screens. And when our radar screens blink, the unknown unknowns now stare us in the face, allowing us to better mitigate risk and do the right thing.

Final Thoughts

Culture is changing. Employees are now searching for purpose and meaning that were before relegated to traditional institutions. Those institutions are losing members in significant numbers and are not sure why. I don't believe it is because the inner desire for purpose, meaning, and growth have faded. I believe it is because culture is changing its default. Easy and simplistic answers are no longer enough. We are recognizing there is meaning in the mess that was previously swept under the rug for the sake of clarity. Those who have left the traditional institutions now make up the largest denomination—the "Nones." They are the self-proclaimed nonaffiliated who make up between 24 and 31 percent of the American population and are searching for community.

There is an opportunity for companies to become this community. All it takes is awareness and a mutual recognition that we are the victims in the street calling out to the bystanders and the coteachers for each other in the mutual search for radar expansion and DTRT.

In the search for DTRT, there is no ingredient more important than the company you keep. What is your company, and is it a place that those who are searching for growth and meaning will want to keep?

Bibliography

Chitale, Radha. "How Could People Watch Alleged Gang Rape 'Like an Exhibit'?" *ABC News*, October 30, 2009. https://abcnews.go.com/Health/MindMoodNews/bystanders-teen-raped/story?id=8948465.

Kelly, Jack. "Wells Fargo Forced to Pay $3 Billion For the Bank's Fake Account Scandal." *Forbes*, February 24, 2020. https://www.forbes.com/sites/jackkelly/2020/02/24/wells-fargo-forced-to-pay-3-billion-for-the-banks-fake-account-scandal/#38c352b342d2.

Kristof, Nicholas. "She Helped a Customer in Need. Then U.S. Bank Fired Her." *New York Times*, February 1, 2020. https://www.nytimes.com/2020/02/01/opinion/sunday/us-bank-fired-employee.html.

Ochs, Susan M. "The Leadership Blind Spots at Wells Fargo," *Harvard Business Review*, October 6, 2016. https://hbr.org/2016/10/the-leadership-blind-spots-at-wells-fargo.

Ramstad, Evan. "U.S. Bank CEO Reviews Firing of Two Employees—and Rules They Broke to Help Customer." *Minneapolis Star Tribune*, February 3, 2020. https://www.startribune.com/u-s-bank-ceo-reviews-firing-of-two-employees-and-of-rule-they-broke-to-help-customer/567524962/.

Sapolsky, Robert M. *Behave: The Biology of Humans at Our Best and Worst.* New York: Penguin Press, 2017.

Schafer, Lee. "Three years on, the Wells Fargo scandal is still breathtaking." *Minneapolis Star Tribune*, January 25, 2020. https://www.startribune.com/schafer-three-years-on-the-wells-fargo-scandal-is-still-breathtaking/567272972/.

Sweet, Ken and Stephanie Dazio. "Wells Fargo to Pay $3 billion Over Fake-Account Scandal." *Associated Press*, February 21, 2020. https://apnews.com/b5fd960b 22a95d59 68f6781f 786ac754.

Wikipedia, s.v. "Bystander effect," last modified 28 April 2020, 11:05, https://en.wikipedia.org/wiki/Bystander_effect.

Wikipedia, s.v. "Irrelegion in the United States," last modified May 5, 2020, 14:49, https://wikipedia.org/wiki/irreligion in the United States.

Wikipedia, s.v. "Milgram experiment," last modified 27 April 2020,17:01,https://en.wikipedia.org/wiki/Milgram_experiment.

Zimbardo, Philip G. *The Lucifer Effect: Understanding How Good People Turn Evil.* New York: Random House, 2007.

About the Author

Timothy R. Velner has been an attorney for over twenty-five years managing transactions, litigation and disputes at various law firms, companies and clinics ranging from a division of the largest privately held corporation in the United States to the Legal Aid Society. In late 1990s he took a brief hiatus to study religion and spirituality at the Graduate Theological Union in

Berkeley, California. Through this unique experience and his capacity to see first-hand when things go wrong, he has distilled commonality to risk and how it can be mitigated through awareness. He combines his knowledge of law and spirituality with anecdotal life experiences, social psychology and philosophy to provide the reader twenty-six practical tools to flesh out the unknowns and do the right thing.